D1610934

GROWING HEALTHY
FRUIT
IN SPAIN

From strawberries to oranges and watermelons

By Clodagh and Dick Handscombe

SANTANA BOOKS

Copyright © 2007 Clodagh and Dick Handscombe
The authors assert the moral right to be identified as the authors
of this work.

Designed by Chris Fajardo
Illustrations by the authors with artwork for chart of
holistic gardening by Lynne Godfrey, sketches for grafting
methods by Patricia Philson, peach tree photographs in section
2.2 by Chris Morgan, baby avocado tree in section 4.14 by
Kitty Wells, palm weevil in section 5.7 by Alicante Department
of Agriculture, back cover photograph by Peter Gudgeon.

'Growing Healthy Fruit in Spain'
is published by Ediciones Santana S.L.
Apartado 41, 29650 Mijas-Pueblo (Málaga) Spain
Telephone: (0034) 952 48 58 38 - Fax: (0034) 952 48 53 67
e-mail: info@santanabooks.com

All rights reserved. No part of this book may be reproduced
or transmitted in any form or by any means without the prior
written permission of the publisher and author.

Printed in Spain by Grafisur

Depósito legal: CA-166-07
ISBN: 978-84-89954-62-5

Where electronic addresses of useful organisations are mentioned
they were correct at the time the book went to press. Their
inclusion by the authors does not imply that the publishers endorse
their services or products. Likewise, where practical solutions to
problems are given there is no guarantee by the publishers or
authors that they will be appropriate or work in every situation.

DEDICATION

To the many amateur gardeners in Spain interested in growing at least some of their own fruit as the basis for healthy eating for themselves and family whether they live in a small apartment, town house, villa, farmhouse or country estate.

We hope that this compendium of ideas, advice and information helps you grow an interesting and healthy diversity of fruit, whether on a mini or large scale, and that you thoroughly enjoy your Spanish harvests fresh from the tree, bush or plant: in salads, cooked, juiced, dried, bottled, frozen, or processed as jams, chutneys, and pickles, or as soft and alcoholic drinks.

ACKNOWLEDGEMENTS

This book would not have been so rich but for the host of good friends and acquaintances — both Spanish and of other nationalities living in Spain — who shared their memories and experiences of past, current and emerging practices related to the growing of fruit and their use in preparing wholesome, appetising and healthy family foods. There are many and for fear of leaving one out by mistake we thank all jointly for their support of our at times way-out (compared with local Spanish tradition) varieties and practices.

CONTENTS

INTRODUCTION

Growing healthy fruit in Spain and its sister book *Growing healthy vegetables in Spain* were written to help you cultivate your own produce from today. This is now possible for all — whether living in a villa, finca, town house, penthouse or the smallest apartment. Amazingly, neither fruit nor vegetables need more than a square metre of space to start. Fruit does not have to be grown in traditional orchards. Today's possibilities include strawberry barrels, containers, tubs, and raised beds that can be accommodated on apartment terraces, in town house patios and corners of any garden. In addition fruit trees can be fitted into flower gardens for their blossom as much as for their fruit. Most importantly, none of the above requires much time.

We give guidelines for each and other more traditional methods within this new-style gardening book. Everyone worldwide is bombarded with propaganda promoting the concept "Eat more fresh vegetables and fruit to improve your health", but there is no comprehensive book in English that tells you how to grow your own fruit under Spanish conditions and harvest them when at their best. Also, since organically produced fruit is more difficult to buy than in the UK and other northern European countries, we emphasise natural, ecological and organic growing methods.

When we first came to Spain 20 years ago we soon found the climate, soil, seeds and trees very different to those we had experienced before. Over the years we have learned much the hard way in expanding our vegetable and fruit growing from small beginnings. We started in a relatively small garden, then borrowed land to expand our fruit and vegetable growing, initially to 400 and then 800 square metres. We are now very self-sufficient and harvest for our daily needs 365 days a year. Surplus fruit crops are frozen, juiced, bottled, dried, converted into chutneys and jams or pickled along with the annual olive crop.

Today many of our most satisfying days in Spain are when we are working on the combined fruit and vegetable plot, harvesting crops when at their best. Then home to eat well al fresco on most nights of the year, enjoying the delights of our flower garden. Perhaps an interesting spread of fruit-based tapas, home-reared rabbit cooked with home-grown apricots, figs or raisins or fish marinated in lemon juice, a bowl of freshly picked raspberries and a home-made wine and fruit liquor.

So with more than a joint century of fruit growing behind us, almost 40 of them in Spain, we are pleased to be able to share our experiences and ideas with you in a way that goes beyond what we have been able to communicate in columns in various newspapers and magazines in Spain and the UK.

The book is structured in six parts:

PART ONE - Your opportunities and benefits
PART TWO - How to grow your own fruit on a mini scale
PART THREE - Expanding the number of fruit trees and plants
PART FOUR - What can be grown, where and how?
PART FIVE - Preventing and controlling problems
PART SIX - A fruit-growing calendar

These are followed by a comprehensive English–Spanish vocabulary.

Each part is subdivided into manageable sections. The contents of each are practical, designed to be easy to understand and follow. We have aimed to offer something useful to everyone: those who have never grown fruit before, those who used to and are thinking of starting again, those with limited experience interested in improving, and those with considerable experience prepared to extend their efforts. With special emphasis on the problems of growing fruit in Spain.

Although this book is about growing and using your own fruit, it is not a vegetarian book. Rather it is designed to be of benefit to everyone moving to, or already living in Spain, whatever their style of eating. Quality fresh fruit, especially if produced naturally, ecologically and organically, should be of interest to the following groups:

- Those who want but have difficulty finding fresh organic fruit.
- Those who already have a reasonably balanced diet based on the traditional Mediterranean diet rich in fresh vegetables and fruit but are interested in a fresher, more diverse source of vegetables and fruit.
- Those beginning to recognise that they are eating too many pre-processed/ manufactured fast foods and that a move to eating more natural, living "slow foods" would be a beneficial first step.
- Those who claim their lifestyles are too rushed to prepare healthy meals but would like to eat more vegetables and fruit to accompany their processed main courses.
- Committed vegetarians or vegans who recognise that in many retail outlets fruit and vegetables are not as fresh and ripe as they used to be in the best village stores and local markets
- Anyone in the above groups who is concerned that more and more fruits and vegetables sold in supermarkets, whether from Spain or imported, is grown under plastic.

We sincerely hope that *Growing healthy fruit in Spain* and *Growing healthy vegetables in Spain* will encourage you to grow and enjoy more home-grown fruit and vegetables wherever you live.

Already we are encouraged. Even though the younger generation is allowing once-productive traditional orchards and allotments handed down over generations to wither away, many expatriate and Spanish neighbours who have retired to our inland valley from working lives in towns and cities are growing their own. Hopefully such new horticulturists will lead the way in re-establishing the best of the once-traditional Mediterranean gardens/ smallholdings, orchards and healthy diet.

Perhaps never in the history of mankind has there been such a need for people of all ages to return to an element of self-sufficiency for the good of their health and enjoyment of life.

— *Clodagh and Dick, 2007.*

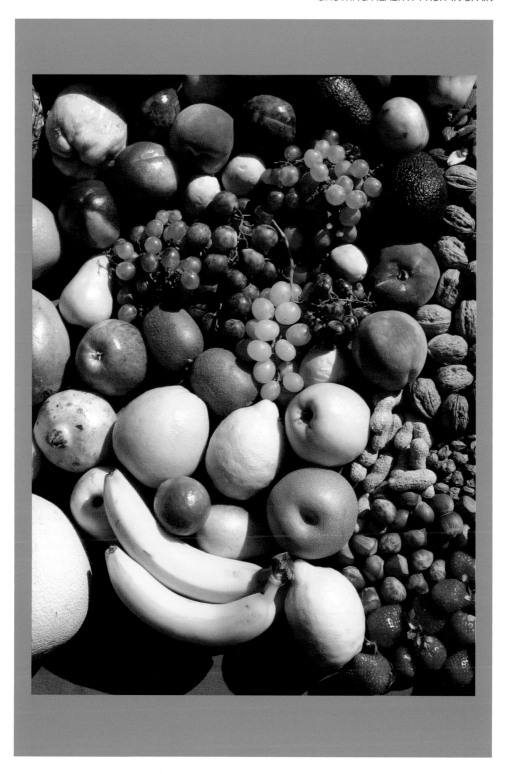

PART ONE

YOUR OPPORTUNITIES AND BENEFITS

There are good reasons why everyone with a property in Spain - even if only visiting for holidays - should grow at least some of their own fruit. The benefits discussed in the following sections are unquestionable so why not start today, even if only on a small scale? You don't even need to have good soil or an abundance of water to have a go. The rest of the book will tell you how.

1.1 THE GREAT OPPORTUNITIES FOR GROWING YOUR OWN

Wouldn't you like to be able to harvest your own fresh fruit up to 365 days a year with relatively little effort? Your favourite fruits harvested when at their best and in quantities you can readily consume before they lose their freshness?

It is certainly possible wherever you live in Spain. An amazing range of fruits grow well, especially if you live along the Mediterranean coast or in nearby inland valleys. By choosing just a few varieties it is possible to harvest fresh fruit on every day of the year, as illustrated in the table below. As explained in Parts Two and Three, you don't need the space for a formal orchard as mini trees, even oranges and lemons, are available that can be grown in containers on apartment terraces or trained on the walls of small patio gardens. And a strawberry barrel or standard grape vine takes up very little space.

TYPICAL HARVEST TIMES - MONTHS

	S	O	N	D	J	F	M	A	M	J	J	A
Lemons	*	*	*	*	*	*	*	*	*	*	*	*
Oranges			*	*	*	*	*	*	*	*		
Mandarins		*	*	*	*	*	*	*	*			
Strawberries				*	*	*	*	*	*	*		
Cherries									*	*		
Apricots										*		
Plums										*	*	
Almonds												*
Grapes	*	*										*
Pears	*											*
Persimmons		*	*	*	*							
Olives			*	*	*							

Naturally, the more space you can allocate to growing fruit the greater the diversity you will have for an interesting and healthy diet. Even the small selection above provides opportunities for eating fruit fresh, drinking fresh juices or incorporating in an amazing range of tapas, salads and cooked dishes.

Whether you start on a mini or large scale, developments in plant breeding, seeds, organic composts, containers, irrigation systems, natural versus chemical fertilisers, insecticides and fungicides are making it easier and safer for even the totally inexperienced to grow good fruit without too much heartache and effort. It is therefore possible to involve children in the activities to encourage them to eat more fruit and vegetables, help them better understand some of their science and environmental lessons and give positive support to "eat well" promotions in the schools.

From cover to cover this book provides step-by-step practical guidelines for the growing of fruit in a wide variety of situations. Mini fruit growing in a space of just one or two square metres is covered in Part Two, and on a larger scale in Part Three. In Part Four we describe more than 60 types of fruit that can be grown, climatic conditions allowing. There is therefore no need for gastronomic boredom.

Our earlier book *Your garden in Spain* includes a chapter entitled *Painting with plants* to demonstrate what can be achieved by planting different decorative plant combinations using the colours of the painter's palette. There are parallels in the use of flowering fruit trees, which can be used to provide protection for the more delicate vegetables and flowering plants.

The leaves, trunks, flowers, fruits and shapes of fruit trees come in an amazingly wide range of colours. Fruit trees are among the earliest flowering trees. And the dying leaves of deciduous fruit trees can give wonderful autumn displays. So it makes sense to incorporate fruit trees within the flower garden or around a vegetable plot.

Growing your own has other advantages

Firstly, you are able to eat fruit at their best, season by season, knowing there is always a new delicious crop just around the corner.

Secondly, since your labour is free, you can avoid the high price mark-ups between growers and retail outlets. Recent press reports indicate that basic commodity fruits are marked up astronomically, e.g. lemons seventeen times the price paid to the grower, oranges five times and mandarins thirty times. The retail price of out-of-season produce or early cherries can be even higher, especially if grown organically.

Thirdly, you will be able to guarantee yourself locally grown produce even when more and more fruit-growing land surrounding villages and towns is being abandoned or sold for development. At a recent European Union-funded citrus fruit-growing course, all the participants except Dick were Spaniards who knew that when they died nobody in their families would continue to work their fields and orchards. Within a few years much of the fruit available in Spanish greengrocers and supermarkets could become imported.

Fourthly, as outlined in section 1.3, your fruit will be grown in the open air rather than in the insecticide environment of the greenhouses now increasingly used to force such fruits as *nísperos*, strawberries and bananas to ripen earlier.

Fifthly, the diversity of fruit colours, flavours, aromas and textures offer the garde-ner-cook a multi-dimensional pallet, allowing him/her to prepare and display food that not only smells and tastes good but looks good. This can be achieved without having to rely on E- additive flavour and colour-enhancers or packaged sauces.

Overall, growing your own fruit can be the route to more satisfying as well as more healthy food, as illustrated in the diagram below.

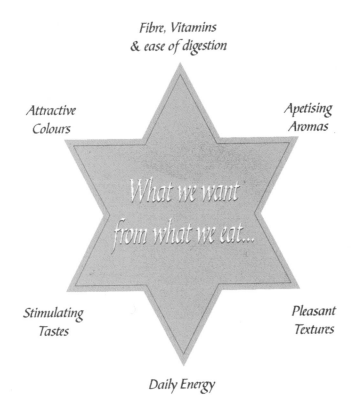

Fibre, Vitamins
& ease of digestion

Attractive
Colours

Apetising
Aromas

What we want
from what we eat...

Stimulating
Tastes

Pleasant
Textures

Daily Energy

1.2 THE DIETARY AND HEALTH BENEFITS FROM GROWING YOUR OWN

Information from government and health institutions indicates that most people would benefit healthwise from eating more fresh fruit and vegetables on a day-to-day basis. Acting on this evidence, many government health departments have launched campaigns to encourage everyone to take positive steps to do so. Spain and the USA are among the many countries encouraging people to eat a minimum of five portions a day of fresh fruit and vegetables to ensure the consumption of a healthy input of fresh vitamins, minerals and fibre each day.

The flow of new diet and health books encouraging greater eating of vegetables and fruit is endless. Common denominators include these points:

- The original Mediterranean diet consisted of fresh vegetables, fruit, herbs and olive oil with fresh fish from an unpolluted Mediterranean sea and rivers and meat from naturally foraged animals and birds.
- In the past 50 years the Mediterranean diet has been unhealthily modified as a result of many people moving to the cities, rushed lifestyles, and the advent of convenience and snack foods.
- Fresh water, vegetables, herbs, fruit and fresh air are the healthiest five ingredients of any diet.
- The greater the diversity and skillful mixing of fresh vegetables and fruit alone or with fish or meat the more likely a meal will be satisfying, healthy and enjoyable.
- Old-fashioned seasonal variations in vegetables and fruit meant one enjoyed what was around at the time and relished the next crops that would be available. Today, when everything is available every day, menus can become standardised and boring.
- The best between-meal nibbles are living snacks, such as a fresh juicy apple, banana, grapes or walnuts.
- The flavours and colourings of fresh fruit and vegetables and fruit are more healthy than manufactured substitutes.
- Fresh fruit juice from juicy sun-ripened fruit is likely to be more beneficial than juice in cartons produced from imported concentrates with added sweeteners.

Fresh fruit and vegetables are the best source of energy, carbohydrates, protein, vitamins, oils and anti-oxidants. Unfortunately, most of the campaigns exhorting us to eat more of these miss out two important points: what is truly fresh and where do you obtain the diversity.

From our experience the freshest fruits are those picked directly from your trees or bushes a few minutes before eating them. The second freshest are those picked early morning for sale at a farm gate, in a local fresh food market or local village store.

And the least fresh? Those purchased prepacked at the end of several days on the shelf, which can be up to a week or longer for some fruits. Although "use by" labels indicate dates before which fruit should be eaten, they do not indicate when they were picked. Some fruit packs now have labels that indicate the state of ripeness based on gases omitted by the fruit, but they do not indicate the fruit's age nor whether they were fresh-picked a few days ago or have been stored - possibly for months - in an air-conditioned chamber. Innovative

technology means chemical treatments can enhance the colour, shine, anti-bruising and keeping qualities of fruit, whether grown in the fresh air ripened by the sun or grown in large
hothouses in an artificial atmosphere.

Few retail outlets sell the full range of seasonal varieties that can be grown or necessarily the tastiest varieties. Some local governments in Spain are planning to reopen daily
municipal fruit and vegetable markets to enable local growers to get produce to the consumer
faster than via supermarket distribution channels and to achieve higher incomes than selling
at very low prices to wholesale distributors. However, there is no guarantee the produce will
be grown naturally, ecologically and healthily.

One aim of the world wide "slow food" movement (www.slowfood.it) is to stimulate
an improvement in gastronomy by revitalising the small-scale domestic ecological production
of fruit, vegetables etc.

Overall message? It's about time we took responsibility for our health through sensible
eating and exercise - and growing one's own fruit can go a long way to providing the basis
for this. This does not necessarily mean having the large allotments or orchards. Many fruits
can be grown in small areas - even in only one square metre. How to do so is explained in
Part Two.

1.3 THE EXTRA BENEFITS FROM GROWING FRUIT NATURALLY, ECOLOGICALLY AND ORGANICALLY

We have grown fruit all our lives and, having started by improving soils with natural fertilisers, it has always seemed sensible to seek out natural manures rather than using manufactured inorganic fertilisers.

A number of factors have stimulated our desire to expand our fruit growing without using manufactured chemicals:

• The desire to be in control and knowledgeable about what products are used in their growing and to ensure that they are friendly to the environment and, most critically, the persons eating the fruit.

• To be able to eat ripe healthy fruit directly from the tree or plant without fear of residual chemical in the skin.

• The absence of any obvious benefits from switching to manufactured inorganic, synthesised products, other than perhaps producing larger trees and higher yields which would be too much for the family to eat.

• Seeing persons dressed in space suits spraying their fruit trees with chemical insecticides and fungicides indicates the health risks and the dangers to surrounding crops and passers-by.

• A nearby smallholder sprayed his vegetable plot with a chemical then flooded

his land to get it into the soil. Within an hour the surface was covered with thousands of dead earthworms, the very things needed to build up a rich, fertile soil. Even worse: in the process he killed very few cut and eel worms, his intended target.

• Locals tried to persuade us to use a canister of fumigating gas to kill off all the organisms and insects on our land to prevent major plagues and pest problems. We didn't follow their advice and have never had major soil-

based problems. Natural methods have speedily solved any problems.

• Before EU regulations required all chemical products to be kept in airtight rooms, smell and fumes pervaded many local agricultural cooperatives. But the number of alternative products labelled as natural, ecological, biological or organic is increasing annually.

• An increasing proportion of Spain's exports of fruit and vegetables to northern Europe are labelled as organically produced and an EU organic product label is to be introduced.

• Both major and niche producers of fertilisers, insecticides and fungicides now offer a full range of ecological and organic alternatives to chemical products.

• More and more organic produce is being sold in Spain, although not to the extent as in many other EU countries.

• Concerns are emerging that some of the chemicals used to keep whole salad vegetables and fruits crisp by reducing water losses may contribute to the increasing obesity of national populations.

• Extensive popular and scientific writings and EU/national government schemes that extol agriculturalists and householders to produce and consume more fresh ecologically/organically produced fruit and vegetables.

• Many fruits and vegetables sold as organic were not crisp and lacked flavour after being on the shelf too long in small health shops due to their high relative prices, only one delivery weekly and lack of meaningful promotion.

• The amazing reappearance of beneficial insects and small animals after converting land previously worked with chemical products to an ecological/organic plot. Dead sterile soil can soon again become "live".

1.4 ENCOURAGING CHILDREN TO GROW AND EAT FRUIT

World wide there is a growing concern about the inadequate quantities of fresh fruit and vegetables children eat and the possible effects on their ability to grow, exercise, study healthily and avoid obesity.

A growing number of countries, including Spain, have programmes for developing a knowledge of the benefits of fruit and vegetables and some schools now include school gardens as one of their group activities.

However, as such initiatives are not universal, it is important for parents and/or grandparents to take the lead. The following practical experiences related to fruit could help young children considerably in their understanding of early science and botany lessons at school.

Smelling things such as ripe strawberries, raspberries, oranges and nectarines.
Picking and dissecting things such as a pomegranate or mandarin.
Sowing and tending strawberry seeds and seedlings until they can be planted out.
Seeing the speed at which an avocado stone can germinate and grow into a tree.
Planting and caring for a patch or barrel of strawberries.

Tending for a dwarf pomegranate or kumquat tree throughout the year.

Drying nuts, apricots, apple slices, strawberries etc. for healthy snacks.

Painting a bowl of fresh fruit.

Labelling fruit trees with long-lasting labels indicating their English, Spanish and botanical names and their planting dates.

Preparing their own fruit salad with their fruit from their own grapevine, strawberry barrel and dwarf apple tree.

Making a refreshing infusion of slices of lemon or orange; or natural ice lollies from pureed raspberries, strawberries and mandarin juice.

Growing a melon for weight or a pineapple from the cut-off top of a purchased pineapple. The latter can be a real challenge.

Help in the harvesting of soft and other fruits and noting the difference between ripe, juicy tasty fruit and hard, unattractive unripe fruit.

Juicing fruit for fresh drinks and home-made ice lollies.

Learning by doing, asking questions, being coached by an elder and achieving personal success at any early age is the best way of developing beneficial beliefs and skills for life.

For birthday, Christmas or *Los Reyes* presents, why not purchase books and games that have a fruit and vegetable theme or mini shops and kitchens that have good reproductions of fruit and associated vegetables included? Such things already exist, but there is a big market opportunity for an entrepreneur in this field.

1.5 THE BASIC SUCCESS FACTORS

From our experience there are 10 basic success factors, each achievable with a little dedication and effort. But, if you don't see yourself meeting all 10, don't lose heart - even achieving some of them can be progress towards an improved diet and health.

1. Start small and selectively.

2. Expand when you have the time, motivation, and perhaps family support to make the home-growing of fruit a priority.

3. Plant what you like to eat or did before being tempted by pre-packed unripe fruit.

4. Use whatever space you can allocate as productively as possible.

5. Be tempted by the benefits of diversity and try out some new varieties each year.

6. Go ecological/organic from Day One.

7. Recognise that growing healthy fruit can become more than a mere hobby as the benefits soon impact all aspects of your lifestyle in Spain, regardless of age.

8. Be economical with the use of water and fertilisers. Not just to save money but to grow your produce naturally.

9. Create a sheltered garden environment. Fruit trees, like humans, don't always enjoy the extremes of the Spanish climate.

10. If it takes up too much time, evaluate why. It doesn't need to.

1.6 BENEFITS OF A TOTAL OR HOLISTIC APPROACH TO GARDENING

Spain's greatest climatic advantage is that it offers the chance to design and develop gardens for living in rather than looking at through the window, as is often the case in cooler, wetter climes. Gardens can match intended outdoor lifestyles in all respects.

OUR FRAMEWORK FOR HOLISTIC GARDENING

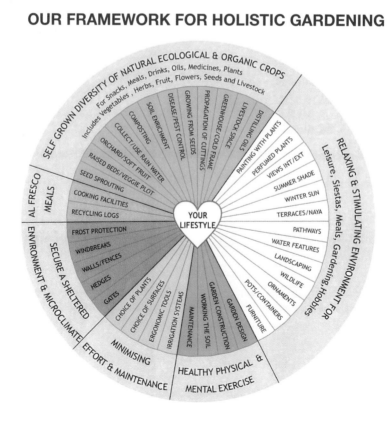

In the diagram we present our new concept of total or holistic gardening. The outer circle summarises the principal objectives or needs for the development of a satisfying, Spanish-lifestyle garden and the inner circle the main elements involved in designing and developing a garden to match.

This book concentrates on how you can move towards achieving the top objective through the growing of a diversity of home-grown fruit. The sister book *Growing healthy vegetables in Spain* does the same in relation to vegetables.

As you progress through the rest of the book you will recognise that almost all the inner elements, not only those in the top bright green segment are important in doing so. They do not apply solely to the development of the flower garden.

Like many, we started out with a bare, uninviting building site but with a vision of what we wanted our Garden of Eden to eventually look like. Early on, the beginning of a now-extensive herb collection was planted, plus a few easy-to-raise fruit and vegetables. Once retired, we had the time to work on expanding the fruit and vegetable garden and keep a few hens, rabbits and snails. These provided sources of light protein to eat with our expanding diversity of vegetables, fruit and edible herbs and also to provide natural fertilisers. Introducing fruit trees, herbs and in the vegetable garden companion plants helped attract wildlife back. It changed from being a sterile piece of ground to an energetic, ecologically friendly, restful place to live.

We learned by our mistakes but this has enabled us to crystallise our vision of a total or holistic garden for the benefit of others. Daily we reap the benefits, related to our physical, mental and bodily health and overall enjoyment of our "retirement". A retirement that is satisfying because it is based on recycling to things we enjoyed doing or had a taste of at various stages of our lives but were constrained from doing to the full by educational demands, family responsibilities, time, or money.

HOW TO GROW YOUR FRUIT ON A MINI SCALE

Part Two presents a range of practical ideas for growing a diversity of fruit on a mini scale - you will be amazed at what can be achieved in a space of less than one square metre especially if you are living in an apartment or small town house. The various sections explain how.

Kumquats

2.1 WHAT DO WE MEAN BY MINI SCALE

By mini we mean ways of growing delicious fruit in areas of only one or two square metres of ground or even less. Yes, even areas as small as your washing up bowl or two pages of your daily newspaper. That's all it needs to grow such things as strawberries, grapes, kiwis, pineapples, a wide variety of fruits on trees with dwarf rootstocks and even a banana plant. So the growing of healthy fruit free of chemical pesticides and wax protection becomes feasible even for those in apartments or small town houses. Naturally you won't have the great harvests possible with an orchard, but you'll have sufficient to enrich a few meals, for snacks, and to delight your taste buds. The possibilities described in the following sections require little time, no expensive tools and no prior experience.

2.2 SOUNDS GREAT - HOW DO I MAKE A START?

A wide range of possibilities are offered to you in the sections that follow. Although designed for persons with little time and space, they can also be used by others with larger gardens but without the motivation or strength to plant and care for fruit trees, bushes and plants within a garden or a mini orchard.

The following success factors are easy to achieve:
• Buy good-quality deep window boxes, containers, planters, etc.

- Buy a rich, water-absorbing but free-draining compost
- Buy good trees, bushes or plants
- Keep the roots damp
- Feed monthly
- Prune once or twice a year as necessary

Parts Four and Five will provide all the support you need in these respects.

Strawberry pot

Tangerine

Peach tree in pot

The crop

2.3 HOW TO GROW FRUIT IN WINDOW BOXES

Window boxes are large enough to plant a few regular or Alpine strawberry plants, blueberries, or miniature pomegranate trees. The yield will not be large, but they add interest and the limited fruits will be relished if living in a small apartment. Fill with a compost mix along the lines of section 2.4b and ensure that this is kept damp at all times. Look out for window boxes which have built-in water reservoirs and a float indicating when the reservoir needs topping up. Window boxes situated on west and east-facing terraces will dry out more slowly than those facing south. Remember: on a north-facing terrace there may not be sufficient sun to develop and ripen fruit. Feed window boxes fortnightly with a dilute nitrogen feed until flower buds form and then switch over to a feed high in potassium as well as nitrogen (see 2.4 below and section 5.3).

2.4 HOW TO GROW FRUIT IN CONTAINERS

A good selection of fruit can be grown in large pots or containers on penthouse and apartment terraces, on roof terraces and within walled patio gardens. Good trees to start with are lemons, mandarins, kumquats, peaches and figs. The lunar and four seasons varieties of lemon tree flower several times a year and can therefore provide a perpetual supply of lemons. Interestingly, fig trees fruit particularly well when their roots are restricted. Grape and kiwis are other alternatives if you want something to train up a wall or over a porch or gazebo to give summer shade on the terrace.

Imagine just reaching up at the end of an August or September dinner and picking a bunch of grapes from above your head to go with the cheese. Grapes can also be trained up poles as standards with a two-metre trunk. Fruiting shrubs such as redcurrants and blueberries can also be grown in containers as well as pineapples bought or self-grown. However, the latter requires two years' patience, no frost and a little luck.

Watch out for terra cotta, plastic or wooden strawberry barrels. The more planting holes there are for plants the better. Stop the lower planted plants from drying out by pushing 5cm-diameter watering tubes down through the compost to the mid-height and bottom of the barrels.

If you love soft fruit, redcurrants and blackcurrants can be grown in containers but you will only get one crop a year so we wouldn't make this a priority if you are short of space. Raspberries would be more productive, producing fruit for up to six months of the year. However, as described in section 3.3, there is no reason you cannot grow a small orchard and collection of soft fruits entirely in large containers.

The success factors for their use are outlined below.

a. Choice of what to grow
You will find it easiest to make a success of mini-scale fruit-growing if you purchase varieties that you like, are suitable for your microclimate, are naturally small or can be purchased in a dwarf variety. You will find many among the 70 types of fruit trees, shrubs and plants listed in Part Four. Some, such as apples and citrus, can sometimes be purchased with two to four varieties of fruit grafted on a single rootstock. If you cannot trace them, have a go at grafting a multi-fruited tree yourself (see section 4.13).

Strawberry barrel

Kumquats

Olive tree in tub

b. Dimensions of container used

A container's diameter or width and depth needs to be sufficient to allow a widening root ball to develop for at least three years before it is moved to a larger one. It must also be deep enough to allow roots to grow downwards, not just around the circumference of the container wall, and to provide a good reservoir of moisture, particularly in the summer months and hot spells at other times.

c. Quality of soil

This is critical. We suggest the following mixes to produce a rich, loamy growing medium which is full of essential nutrients and water-absorbing/retaining while at the same time being free-draining. The latter is important as trees do not like to be waterlogged.

If you have access to garden soil, make up a 1:2:1 mix of compost, earth and well-rotted loose or bagged manure. If not, mix a bag of soil-based compost with a bag of compost which is animal manure-based but with a high compost content.

Recognise that soft fruits such as strawberries and blueberries require a more acid soil than most fruit trees so use a bag of compost especially prepared for acid-loving plants.

d. Supplementary monthly feeds

As your fruit trees, bushes and plants grow, they will gradually use up the nutrients in the soil so it will be necessary to start to feed them during the second spring when leaf and fruit buds are starting to open. Guidelines are provided in section 5.3. A very useful feed is the liquid one can drain from a small domestic worm composter (see section 5.6).

e. Watering

Keep the soil in the containers just damp at all times. Daily watering may be required during hot weather while once a week may suffice during cooler winter spells. If you are always at home, a few containers can be easily watered with a watering can or hose. However, if you are likely to be away or forget to water every so often, we recommend that you construct a mini drip-irrigation system. Luckily small kits are now available. The addition of a water-absorbing gel such as Terracotem (www.terravida.com) to the bottom half of the soil will help maintain a constant water reservoir and slow down the drying of the soil should there be a fault in the irrigation system (see section 4.11). Trees in containers also benefit from a weekly mist spray of their leaves with water.

f. Pest and disease control

Pests and diseases are often caused by under and over-watering, so take care in this respect. Spray trees preventively every month with neem against various moths and flies and watch out for problems. Section 5.7 provides you with a comprehensive guide to possible problems and their treatments. It also explains what neem is and how it can be purchased.

g. Protection from hot winds

Shade containers during the hottest part of summer days to prevent water evaporation from the leaves and from the surface of the soil. Also keep them away from the exit ducts of central heating systems during the winter to avoid drying out leaves and the premature ripening of semi-formed fruit.

h. Protection from cold winds and frosts

Ensure that containers are sheltered from cold winter winds and frosts. If you believe they are at risk, wrap trees in several layers of fleece or bubble wrap covered with green, woven, wind-break cloth. Remember that an air-conditioning unit emits cold air in the summer. If a lemon tree is placed near the exit air vent, the tree can easily suffer the equivalent of severe frost damage.

i. Harvesting

Aim to harvest when the fruit is at its best and eat fresh or use in salads, deserts, fruit-based drinks or cooked dishes that day. Should you achieve gluts even from one or two trees, bushes or plants, many fruits can be stored for a few days, frozen or dried. This is discussed in section 4.16.

j. Aesthetic appearance of containers

While the appearance of a container in a corner of a garden may not be a big issue, this will not be the case on an apartment/penthouse terrace or in a patio garden. So do choose attractive-looking containers.

k. Manoeuvrability of containers

Containers for trees are going to be heavy once filled with damp soil, so it is wise to place the containers on small trolleys such as those used under gas bottles if you expect to move the containers around at any time. Some large containers come with built-in wheels but they can be rather expensive.

2.5 HOW TO GROW FRUIT IN MINI RAISED BEDS OR PLANTERS

Small raised beds and built-in or movable oblong planters are a convenient, low-commitment, low-cost way to grow a few fruit. They should be regarded as large containers and the same success factors apply. They have advantages over containers or planters in that more can be grown than in a large pot or strawberry barrel.

Some planters come with an attached wooden or plastic back trellis, convenient for supporting grape or kiwi vines, fan peach or nectarine trees or cordon apples, pears or raspberries.

Shallow raised beds of 30cm depth could be used for growing strawberries, but you would be better-off with a productive strawberry barrel which occupies only a third of a square metre.

The success factors are as for containers (see section 2.4 above).

2.6 TRAINED ON HOUSE OR BOUNDARY WALLS

The vertical walls of houses, outbuildings and boundary walls are free space for growing fruit and the trunks take up very little ground space.

The possibilities include:
*   fan and cordon fruit trees such as peaches, nectarines and cherries,
*   cordon trees such as apples and oranges,
*   vines such as grapes, kiwis or passion fruit.

To avoid making numerous holes in the walls for tie rings, the trees and vines can be trained on wires stretched between end rings or posts. Since the roots of trees and vines go deep, more shallow flowering plants or bulbs can be planted 30cm away from the trunks.

Pomegrantes

Mangoes

2.7 TRAINED OVER PORCHES AND GAZEBOS

The trunks of vines such as grapes, kiwis and passion flowers take up very little space so they are good alternatives to flowering climbing shrubs for trailing over porches and gazebos or wires stretched over terraces to give summer shade. These are often seen in Spanish gardens.

2.8 INDIVIDUAL SPECIMENS WITHIN GARDEN

However small your garden, one or two fruit trees can normally be fitted into flower beds, an area of stone chippings or in the centre of a terrace for the spring blossom and/or summer shade as well as the fruit. By careful pruning and the weighting of young branches a cherry, olive or fig tree can be trained to provide a wide, leafy umbrella under which to enjoy a summer lunch or later siesta. Even a mature date palm would only take up a metre of ground space.

The only potential problems are that fallen blossom and fruit need to be cleared from stone chippings or terraces and fallen fruit can stain terrace stone slabs or tiles.

Tropical fruit trees are best grown in beds in front of south-facing walls or in really sheltered south-facing corners, especially if light frosts can be expected.

Even for only one tree we suggest that you first prepare the ground and planting hole as outlined in Part Four.

2.9 TROPICALS IN SHELTERED BEDS AND CORNERS

If you have a really sheltered south-facing wall or corner of the garden facing south, you can attempt to grow a tropical fruit tree such as a banana, papaya, mango or lychee even on the Costa Blanca. Further south it will be even easier. Section 4.6 provides information on the frost hardiness of tropical fruits.

PART THREE

EXPANDING YOUR FRUIT-GROWING – AN ORCHARD IS NOT THE ONLY OPTION

Outlined here are the many places and ways in which growing fruit can be incorporated into gardens of all sizes.

3.1 WHAT ARE THE VIABLE OPTIONS?

There are many ways in which fruit trees, bushes and plants can be incorporated into a garden besides growing them on a mini scale. A number of the most popular and practical ways are described below.

Which you use will depend on the size and shape of your land, the contours of the land, the quality of soil and the availability of compost and well-rotted manures for improving the soil, the overall plan for its utilisation, the numbers of trees, bushes and plants you wish to plant and the style of garden you plan around the house. Above all, you will need good soil for success with most fruits. This is discussed in sections 3.17, 4.2E and 4.10.

You may have purchased a property with a good selection of fruit trees already in the garden or with a sizeable orchard. If you are lucky, the trees will have been well-tended right up to your arrival. On the other hand your property may have been built amid an abandoned orchard with un-pruned trees, dead branches everywhere and signs of stress from not being irrigated for some time.

Don't despair. The trees may recover with appropriate heavy pruning, feeding, watering and perhaps some grafting to produce good harvests within a year or two. Guidelines for pruning, feeding and watering are included in Part Four.

What you will be able to successfully grow is also covered in Part Four. However, at this stage read through the options that follow and decide which would best match your needs in terms of the range and quantities of fruit you would like to harvest each year, the amount of land you have and the quality of the soil.

3.2 JUST EXPAND THE NUMBER OF LARGE CONTAINERS

If you have experimented with growing fruit in a few containers and you achieved good yields, one way to expand is to collect more large containers 60-100cm deep. In theory, there is no limit to the number of fruit trees and fruit bushes and plants that can be grown in containers. Indeed, it may be the only way other than raised beds if your site has shallow or no topsoil, or the soil you have is very stale.

The only factors that might inhibit you from developing a container orchard are the aesthetics and being able to prepare sufficient rich soil/compost/manure mix (see section 2.4).

3.3 A TEN-TUB MINI ORCHARD

The 10-tub concept, first introduced in Growing healthy vegetables in Spain, is a half-way house between a group of containers of mixed sizes and a large raised bed.

The best tubs to use have a diameter of 70 to 120cm and are 70 to 100cm deep, i.e. the type of tub used by garden centres for large flowering trees, olives and palms. They can be purchased from agricultural cooperatives or horticultural suppliers.

This method is especially useful if your garden is bedrock with just a few centimetres of rocky, dusty soil. It could also be used in a large patio or courtyard garden or around a motor home plot.

If we were to establish a 10-tub mini orchard, we would plant them up as follows:

Tub 1: strawberries, with holes in the sides of the tubs for extra plants.
Tub 2: a mandarin tree, the fruit is sweeter than oranges.
Tub 3: a lunar lemon that is perpetual-fruiting.
Tub 4: a peach tree.
Tub 5: an olive tree in order to prepare our own olives for tapas.
Tub 6: a fig tree, preferably a sweet green variety.
Tub 7: an apple tree to eat fruit directly off the tree.
Tub 8: an avocado tree as we like them in salads.
Tub 9: half a dozen raspberry canes that fruit for many months in Spain.
Tub 10: redcurrant and blackcurrant bushes for eating with yogurt.

3.4 LARGER DEDICATED RAISED BEDS

Mini raised beds were mentioned in section 2.5, but in practice raised beds can be of any size. The main requirements are:

Depth: a minimum of 30cm growing strawberries, 60cm for fruit bushes and preferably 80 to 90cm for fruit trees.

Width: a maximum of 75cm across if they can only be worked from one side or 1.5 metres if workable from both sides. This will allow you to weed, grow surrounding plants such as strawberries, trailing grape vines, blueberries or co-planted vegetables without walking on the soil. While the trees are small it is wise to place a plank where you need to walk for pruning and harvesting.

Raised beds can be of any length and sited anywhere within a garden or estate. Also they can be oblong, square, oval or circular - just decide what fits best into the overall garden design. Placed in front of a sunny south-facing wall, they can be an excellent place for growing tropical fruits such as mangoes and bananas.

The walls of raised beds can be built from many materials, but the most aesthetic are generally unrendered natural stone, rendered stone or blocks and bricks. Un-rendered aggregate blocks, old wooden doors or panels and railway sleepers can also be used but look less attractive. See *Growing Healthy Vegetables in Spain* for more information.

The most important thing about raised beds is as for containers: don't take short cuts when filling them. If you don't have a ready supply of good compost and manure, wait until you have found a supply or have produced your own.

3.5 FRUIT TREES PLANTED WITHIN A MIXED GARDEN

Fruit trees can play a major role in a diversely planted mixed garden. As well as providing fruits, some, such as almonds and cherries, are among the first trees to flower in the spring and the ripe fruits of mandarins and oranges can brighten gardens from October through to May. As will be discussed in Section 4.13, many fruit trees can be pruned into a wide variety of architectural shapes designed to fit into small gardens, making it easier to harvest fruits and maximise the amount of shade they give.

When trees are trained as standards, annual and perennial bulbs, shrubs and plants can be planted almost up to the trunk except under shallow-rooted types such as citrus and avocado. Mature cherries, mulberry, chestnuts, walnuts, fig and carob are tall and wide and can be made the centre-piece of moderate-sized gardens or courtyards of larger properties. Place large tables and chairs under their spreading boughs for communal summer eating (except during the month when their fruit is ripening). Cordon and fan trees can be trained on house and boundary walls as well as on wires within the garden to create internal hedges and windbreaks.

Individual or groups of trees can be attractively planted in a lawn or in areas of stone chippings laid over plastic sheeting. The latter usefully reducing the need for watering. Fruit trees such as the avocado and carob can be used to hide the garden shed.

And one should not forget that the date palm is a fruit tree and can make a majestic impact on any garden, whether as a single tree in the front garden, by the pool, or as a small oasis. Lastly, a soft fruit bed is easy to fit in anywhere, if your microclimate is appropriate, whether your favourites are strawberries, raspberries or redcurrants.

3.6 PLANTING FRUIT TREES, BUSHES AND PLANTS WITHIN A COTTAGE-STYLE GARDEN

Within a less formal, wilder, cottage-style garden, dwarf fruit trees, fruit bushes and plants can be attractively intermingled among flowering plants and vegetables. For instance, red and blackcurrants can be mixed into shrub beds, ramblers such as blackberries, loganberries and kiwis can be intertwined with climbing passion flowers and bignonias and strawberries can be grown among low-growing annuals and perennials or hanging over the walls of raised beds.

We have one large shrub bed with a carpet of alpine strawberry plants, originally only 10 plants grown from seed. The plants not only provide delicious fruits but act as a living mulch giving shade to the roots of the shrubs, reducing moisture evaporation and - when the leaves start to wilt - provide a warning that the soil is becoming dry.

3.7 CO-PLANTING FRUIT BUSHES, PLANTS AND TREES AROUND THE VEGETABLE PLOT

If you are in an exposed situation or want to hide the vegetable plot, consider planting a row of fruit trees around the entire edge. These could be pruned as bushes, standards, fans or cordons. Cordons and fans trained on wires can also be planted as internal windbreaks, breaking up the plot into a number of wide strips or squares and providing some summer shade. The

latter is particularly useful for vegetables such as lettuces, chard and spinach that go quickly to seed in hot weather. There will be little competition for nutrients if you plant only shallow-rooted vegetables close to the fruit trees.

Many gardeners, including ourselves, plant their soft fruits alongside one side of the land prepared for vegetables as they have similar needs for rich soils and regular irrigation.

3.8 FRUIT CAGES FOR SOFT FRUITS

If you plan to grow a large number of the soft fruits described in section 4.7 - strawberries, redcurrants, raspberries, etc. - it may be worth investing in a two-metre-high fruit cage within which you can plant and work with the minimum of bird damage and losses. However, our experience is that in most areas of Spain there is still so much natural food available for birds that they are not a major problem. To deter what birds there are, plant a line of sunflowers along the side of an un-netted soft-fruit area.

A fruit cage, which can be anything from three by three metres to 30 by 30 metres, can be fitted in and hidden anywhere in your garden.

3.9 PROTECTING OR REPLANTING HILLSIDE TERRACES

For more than a millennium olives, almonds and grape vines have been grown on hillside terraces. The depth of soil behind each terrace wall is deep enough to retain sufficient moisture during the summer months to sustain the trees. With drip irrigation it is possible to grow a wider range of trees. On the Costa Blanca this would include apples pears and loquats, on the Costa Tropical avocados and mangoes, and in both areas grape vines, almonds and olives. In some cases old trees will be in poor condition and will need replacing after improving the soil.

3.10 PLANTING FRUIT TREES ON STEEP SLOPES

In some inland areas it is not unusual to have one or more steep slopes to cope with, that is slopes with an inclination of 25 to 50 degrees. Rows of fruit trees can be an effective way of covering and stabilising such earth banks and, particularly if citrus fruits, of inhibiting weed growth under the trees. The only potential problem if the trees are allowed to grow large is the pruning and harvesting of the down slope sides of the trees.

3.11 PLANTING FRUIT TREES AS A BOUNDARY HEDGE OR COPSE

Citrus trees and avocado trees planted in single, double or triple rows can provide a thick boundary screen for security and to reduce the noise of passing traffic.

Many deciduous trees can also be used as a single or mix of varieties, but they will not provide a winter screen and tend not to have as many low branches as citrus trees. Naturally one could plant an outer hedge of citrus trees with inner rows of other varieties.

If you want a prickly impenetrable boundary hedge to keep people and large animals out, nothing is more effective than tall prickly pear cacti or sloes. Both have culinary uses. When fully ripe, the prickly pear fruits can be carefully harvested (section 4.4) and eaten fresh, used in cooking or to prepare a liquor. Likewise, sloes are invaluable for preparing a home-made alternative to *pacharán* by merely half-filling a bottle with fruit and then topping up with anise liquor. Since sloes are harvested in August, the drink will be ready to drink by Christmas.

If the property is surrounded by high wire-mesh fences, consider training grapes, passion fruit and kiwis on the fence. Within a few years you will have a good windbreak and screen during the summer months. Unfortunately, the three climbers are deciduous and lose their leaves in the autumn.

3.12 USING FRUIT TREES FOR INTERNAL HEDGES OR WINDBREAKS

Fruit trees on dwarf rootstocks are suitable for use as internal hedges or windbreaks in average-sized gardens. In larger gardens mandarin or orange trees planted two or three metres apart can be attractive. To save space they can be trained as a series of fans or as a line of cordons. Crossing branches in a line of cordons are easily grafted to join each tree to the next. This creates a stronger, more robust hedge.

Tall rows of raspberries and grape, passion fruit and kiwi vines trained on wires can also be used.

3.13 A TRADITIONAL ORCHARD

A traditional orchard can consist of a square, oblong or round copse. Rows of trees are traditionally planted with five to seven metres between the trunks. Five will be sufficient for most bush forms of trees but seven metres will be required if you plan to train trees with wide umbrellas to maximise the effect of the sun on ripening fruit and to make harvesting easier. If you plant a large orchard, recognise that the family is unlikely to be able to use anywhere near the yields of fruit and prices on the wholesale market may be so low that you get little income for your efforts.

Maybe you are one of the increasing number of expatriates purchasing large tracts of orchard land in order to build in an inland rural area. If you are lucky, the trees will be in good shape and you can keep the orchard areas as they are, except for carving out an area for a garden around the house and maybe a secluded pool area.

On the other hand your land may be an abandoned orchard in which many trees have died. In such case some trees can probably be nursed back to health with diligent pruning, watering and feeding. The others will need cutting down to prevent diseases from spreading. As an alternative to replanting, why not develop a meadow with scattered trees into a wild-flower meadow?

47

3.14 SOFT-FRUIT STRIP BEDS WITHIN ORCHARDS OR ELSEWHERE

Fruit trees are normally planted five to seven metres apart (as we have mentioned), so - at least while they are young - it is convenient to grow long, narrow beds of soft fruit between the lines of trees in the same way as vegetables are grown in fruit-growing areas. The possible fruits are discussed in section 4.7. Melons could be grown in the same way as illustrated.

3.15 FRUIT-GROWING FINCAS

If you purchase a large farm comprising many hectares of vines, olives or oranges for rural peace and privacy, the challenge arises of maintaining the hundreds of trees and harvesting the crops. Many will resort to hiring help and joining the local cooperative to be able to pro-

cess their olives to oil and their grapes to wine, and with luck sell their oranges to a juice factory. If you are near an urban area, it may be possible to organise a pick-your-own scheme.

3.16 WALLED GARDENS

Some are fortunate enough to have a large walled courtyard in the centre of a cortijo-style property or a large walled yard that used to be used for animals. In both cases fan and cordon fruit trees and vines can be grown on the entire wall trained on horizontal wires 50cm apart. The most tender fruits will be best grown on the warm south facing-wall and a soft fruit cage could be fitted in against the walls of a sunny corner.

In the centre you could grow strips of vegetables divided by rows of cordon fruit trees. The latter would also provide windbreaks in exposed situations.

3.17 THE SUCCESS FACTOR - YOUR OVERALL GARDEN DESIGN AND NANO CLIMATES

However small or large, limited or diverse, the success of your planned fruit-growing activity will depend on two factors: how aesthetically you are able to fit your favourite fruits into your overall garden design; and, most importantly, the climates within your garden.

You need to take into account three levels: macro, micro and nano climates.

As illustrated in the table, the first you can do nothing about except by moving house, the second you can modify to a degree and the third - the nano climate - is entirely in your hands. How far you control it will determine how successful you will be. The important thing is to realise that the macro and micro climates are both above ground while the nano climate is both above and below ground.

CLIMATIC FEATURES THAT WILL AFFECT GROWTH OF YOUR FRUIT

Macro climate of your geographic area: includes general pattern of annual and seasonal hours of sunshine, temperatures, wind, humidity, rain, frost, hail and snow, and determines the range of fruit trees, bushes and plants your local nurseries will stock.

Micro climate within your specific garden: influenced by the extent, pattern and balance of sunshine, shade, protection from hot and cold drying winds, and beneficial wildlife achieved as a result of your garden's design and the location of your fruit-growing within the overall plan.

Nano climate: the very localised conditions above and below the ground relating to and influencing each specific fruit tree, bush and plant whether planted in containers or within the garden. It is very critical but luckily can be easily improved by yourself.

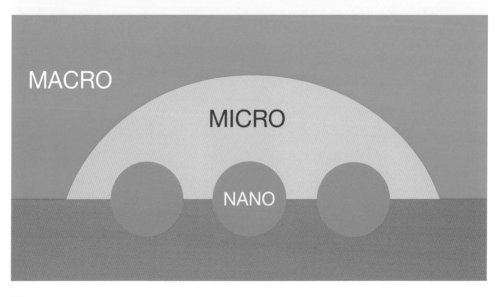

CHARACTERISTICS OF:

POOR NANO CLIMATE

ABOVE GROUND

1. No beneficial insects
2. Constant chemical insecticide/fungicide mist
3. Watering of leaves causing fungal attacks
4. No shade or shelter from hot/cold winds
5. Hard solid soil surface

BELOW GROUND

1. Soil lacks natural nutrients.
2. Soil is compacted solid mass
3. No worms in soil
4. Sterile, stale soil with very few microbes, mostly bad
5. Variable moisture, either dry or waterlogged
6. Roots force fed with fast chemical fertilisers when trees, bushes and plants look stres

GOOD NANO CLIMATE

ABOVE GROUND

1. Beneficial insects, animals and birds
2. Limited natural organic sprays
3. Surface watering except for rain
4. Windbreaks and natural shading
5. Regularly loosened surface soil

BELOW GROUND

1. Natural nutrients available in the soil.
2. Open crumbly aerated soil structure.
3. Large worm population.
4. Full of beneficial microbes.
5. Constant moisture, never waterlogged.
6. Roots able to continually find and extract what they need from the soil.

The first requirement to achieve an optimum nano climate for the fruit you decide to grow is to prepare the soil before starting to plant. You will find this discussed in various sections of Part Four.

PART FOUR

WHAT CAN BE GROWN, WHERE AND HOW

Fruits can be produced in any garden and on any apartment terrace, as explained in Parts One to Three. The following sections provide guidelines for selecting, planting and growing some 70 types that can be grown on the coastal plains, in inland valleys and on mountainsides, provided you have the appropriate micro-climate. Choose the right mix and, within only a couple of years, you can be harvesting your own healthy fruit 365 days a year.

4.1 INTRODUCTION - THE GREAT OPPORTUNITIES

A wide range of temperate, subtropical and tropical fruit can be grown in Spanish gardens and on apartment terraces, as illustrated in Part One (though not all in every garden and on every terrace as the temperatures at which they can thrive and survive vary).

One does not need an enormous selection to be harvesting fresh, vitamin-rich fruit for immediate consumption all year around. For instance, a "lunar" or "four seasons" lemon tree will flower and fruit several times a year making possible continuous harvesting of its fruit. Three varieties of mandarins and oranges - early, mid-season and late - can allow harvesting from October to the end of May. Likewise, raspberries can fruit from May until November and strawberries even longer if some are covered by cloches, enabling them to be harvested from February until Christmas - or with care and a little luck every month of the year.

DECIDING ON THE TYPE AND FORM OF TREES

You have several related decisions to make:

1. Decide the types of fruit you want to grow. This may include your favourites, types difficult to buy when at their best or, if available, are rather expensive, and types you don't really know but would like to try.

2. Decide whether you can provide suitable micro and nano climates for each of these types of fruit. In this respect sections 4.2 to 4.9 describe the conditions required for some 70 types of fruit.

3. Consider the age and form of tree that will best suit the planned size and layout of your garden, orchard or containers etc. Here are your options:

a. Young maiden trees one or two years old with a single trunk that has not yet been pruned to stimulate side branches.
The advantages: you will be able to train the young tree into a cordon, bush or standard etc. as you wish, it should be easier to establish a young tree than a mature tree and the younger the tree the lower the price.
The disadvantages: the tree will make no immediate impact on your garden and you will have to wait a good number of years before a meaningful harvest.

b. Two to four-year-old trees that have been pruned once or several times to create cordon, espalier, bush or standard shapes.
The advantages: you don't have to worry about the initial shaping of the tree, it should have a strong root ball and you will have fewer years to wait for fruit.
The disadvantages: it may take longer to establish the tree in poor soils and the tree will probably cost two to three times that of a maiden tree.
These trees are normally sold in containers but some nurseries sell trees bare-rooted. These are trees dug up from a nursery bed and then just earthed-up in the garden centre until sold with no earth around the roots. If you purchase such trees, be sure that the roots have not been allowed to dry out and have them wrapped in damp hessian

for your journey home. Then put the root balls in a bucket of water for a day before planting.

c. Mature trees eight to 10 years old, or more.

The advantage: you will have an instant specimen which will fruit the first year if it has been carefully pruned and cared for.

The disadvantages: the care required to re-establish the pruned root system, the cost of delivery and the price of the tree, which could be 10 times that of a maiden tree or even hundreds of times if purchasing several 100-year-old olive trees for instance. Also, especially with mature citrus trees, the main branches are often cut back so hard that the tree may not regain its original natural shape.

If you buy mature trees in a large tub, keep it for growing a dwarf tree (see section 3.3) or vegetables.

d. Fifty to two-thousand-year-old trees. Yes, there are date palms up to several hundred years old for sale, and olive trees first planted by the Romans. They cost a few thousand euros each and will take a few years to establish themselves in a new situation.

If you are buying soft fruits, young rooted cuttings or mature container-grown bushes are generally available. Most can be grown as bushes or cordons.

Some of the characteristics of various possible tree buys are illustrated below.

Age of tree	Characteristics	Ease of establishing a good tree	Watering needs in early years - litres per day	Risk of failure
1 year	Few/short roots	High	Low	Medium
2-3 years	Root ball developed	High	Medium	Low
4-5 years	Pruned to final form.Could be rootbound	High	Medium	Low
7-10 years	Roots often pruned to fit into container. Branches may be pruned back	Medium	High	Medium
20-2000 years	Very mature, roots and branches pruned back	Medium *	High	Low/medium*

* Depends on care taken in digging up, storage until sold and delivered, and in transplanting.

Possible shapes and rootstocks	Rootstock	Space required per tree	Potential yields per tree - kilos	Relative water needs	Relative nutrient needs	Relative annual pruning
Bastion	Dwarf	Very low	Low	Low	Low	Low
Cordon	Dwarf	Low	Low	Low	Low	Low
Espalier	Dwarf	Low	Low/medium	Low/medium	Low/medium	Low/medium
Fan	Dwarf	Low/medium	Low/medium	Low/medium	Low/medium	Medium
Bush	Dwarf	Medium	Medium	Medium	Medium	Medium
Bush	Vigorous	High	High	Medium/high	Medium/high	Medium/high
Standard	Dwarf	Medium	Medium	Medium	Low/medium	Low/medium
Standard	Vigorous	High	High	High	High	High

Naturally it is preferable to purchase dwarf trees for planting in containers and in small gardens. The various shapes are illustrated.

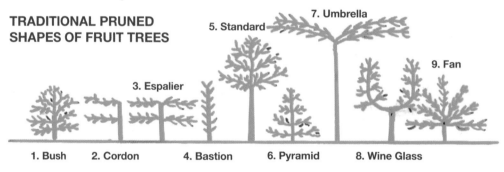

TRADITIONAL PRUNED SHAPES OF FRUIT TREES

7. Umbrella
5. Standard
9. Fan
3. Espalier
1. Bush   2. Cordon   4. Bastion   6. Pyramid   8. Wine Glass

Having decided what to buy, check out a number of garden centres and agricultural cooperatives to see what is available. Check the following before making final decisions:
- What varieties are available? Are those on sale normally grown in the area and if not what precautions should you take to establish them?
- Are the varieties being sold disease-resistant and, if so, to what diseases?
- Are the trees grafted on dwarf or vigorous rootstocks?
- Which specific trees, bushes and plants look the best?

In pots   Bare rooted

A checklist in section 4.2D will help you assess individual trees. Above all, don't purchase trees that show signs of pests and diseases. The labels on fruit trees are often lacking information so you will need to discuss your needs with the nurseryman.

BUT THERE ARE RISKS!

Although the range of fruits that can be grown in the areas where most expatriates are likely to buy properties is wide and the typical average climate ideal, there are several potential problems.

Extremes of temperatures, heavy storms, gales and hail and frost can wreak havoc, especially at blossom time and later in the year just before harvest time. But this won't occur every year, so don't despair.

You may have purchased a plot of land that has been impoverished by the growing of vines or fruit trees for centuries. This can be overcome by improving the soil before replanting.

You may have insufficient domestic or agricultural water to irrigate your fruit trees when they most need it during the spring and summer and early autumn before it rains. If so, restrict the number of trees you plant and plant only those types of trees that are reasonably drought-resistant (see the descriptive charts in sections 4.2 to 4.9).

You may well inherit old trees that have been neglected. You can either prune them heavily and nurse them back to fruiting strength or graft new branches on the old trunk. If the roots are healthy, this could be a quicker route to good healthy crops. For this reason section 4.13 looks at grafting in some detail, including how to produce multi-fruiting trees.

Unfortunately, fruit trees often attract more pests and diseases than vegetable plants so you will need to take preventive actions and react fast if you notice problems. This is particularly true if you live in an area with uncared-for or deserted orchards waiting to be developed. See what can be done in section 5.7.

4.2 CITRUS FRUITS

A. MAIN USES AND BENEFITS

Eat as fresh fruit, juice, include in fruit salads and use juices and rinds in cooking and drinks. Home-made candied peel can be produced for the Christmas cake. Try mandarin or tangerine juice as a pleasant alternative to orange juice when the oranges are not yet fully sun ripened.

B. TYPES OF FRUIT POSSIBLE

The table below summarises the main types of citrus fruit you are likely to find in Spanish gardens. Note: clementines, tangerines and satsumas are derivatives of mandarins by plant breeding.

TYPE OF FRUIT English, Spanish and botanical names	Form	TBT	THT	TPT
ORANGE sweet Naranja *Citrus sinensis*	Tree Bush Cordon	Mar/Apr	Oct/Jun (DP)	Mar
ORANGE bitter Naranja Sevilla *Citrus aurantium*	Tree Bush Cordon	Mar/Apr	Jan/Mar	Mar
MANDARIN Mandarina *Citrus pecticulata*	Tree Bush	Mar/Apr	Dec/May (DP)	Mar
CALAMONDINO Calamondino *Citrofortunela microcarpa*	Tree* Bush*	Mar/Apr	Dec/Mar	Mar
CLEMENTINE Clementina *Citrus clementina*	Tree	Mar/Apr	Sep/Feb	Mar
TANGERINE Tangerina *Citrus tangerina*	Tree	Mar/Apr	Nov/Jan	Mar
SATSUMA Satsuma *Citrus unshiu*	Tree	Mar/Apr	Sep/Jan	Mar
GRAPEFRUIT Pomelo *Citrus paradisi*	Tree	Mar/Apr	Oct/Mar	Mar
LEMON Limón *Citrus limon*	Tree	Perp[++]	Perp[++]	Mar

Grapefruit

Typical planting heights above sea level (metres)				PR	DR	FR
 200	 400	 800	> 1000			
*	*			M	M	M
*				M	M	L/M
*	*			M	M	M
*	*			M	M	M
*	*			M	M	M
*	*			M	M	M/H
*	*			M	M	M/H
*	*			M	M	M/H
*	*			M	M	L/M

TYPE OF FRUIT English, Spanish and botanical names	Form	TBT	THT	TPT
LIME Lima *Citrus aurantifolia*	Tree	Mar/Apr	Oct/Nov	Mar
KUMQUAT Naranja china *Citrus fortunella margarita*	Tree* Bush*	Mar/Apr	Dec/Mar	Mar
LIMEQUAT Lima china *Citrus fortunella*	Tree* Bush*	Mar/Apr	Dec/Mar	Mar

Notes:
TBT = Typical blossom time. **THT** = Typical harvest time. **TPT** = Typical pruning time.
PR = Pest and disease resistance. **DR** = Drought resistance. **FR** = Frost resistance.
H = High. **M** = Medium. **L** = Low.
(DP) = Depending on variety (see table on page 62).
* Small varieties with miniature fruits. Good in containers.
++ Perp = Perpetual flowering/fruiting varieties which flower several times a year and always have fruit at various stages of development on the tree (see table below).
Calomondino, a cross between kumquat and mandarin, bears fruit that look like mini mandarins.

Lemons

Mandarins

Limequat

Typical planting heights above sea level (metres)				PR	DR	FR
 200	 400	 800	> 1000			
*				M	M	L
*	*	*		M	M	M/H
*				M	M	L/M

During the very bad air frosts of February and March 2005, we noticed the following pattern of damage to citrus trees:

Least frost resistant - limes; a little better - lemons; moderate resistance - mandarin, orange and limequat; most resistant - grapefruit, satsuma, kumquat.

At two to three degrees below freezing fruit can become frozen and inedible and the leaves at the tips of branches will be lost. At seven to eight degrees below branches can be seriously damaged and at temperatures lower than 15 degrees below young trees' trunks are likely to be lost (see section 5.1).

Kumquat

Oranges

Grapefruit

Tangerines

C. CHOICE OF VARIETIES

Some typical varieties suitable for garden cultivation are listed. However, recognise that availability can vary according to region and that commercial research stations and nurseries are continually producing new cultivars to achieve improved consistency of fruit size, number of fruit per tree, flavour before fully ripe, consistent colouration, skin thickness and hardness, pest and disease resistance, drought and frost resistance and earlier or later maturity.

Check nurseries, garden centres and agricultural cooperatives to see what varieties are available in your area before making your final choice. Also ask whether dwarf cultivars are available as these will be the most suitable for small town-house gardens or patios and for growing in large pots. Look out especially for disease-resistant cultivars.

If you can't find what you want, ask an agricultural cooperative whether they can place an order for you for spring delivery.

TYPE OF FRUIT	TYPICAL VARIETIES
Mandarin: Mid season Late season	Tangelo, Elindale, Nova Fortuna, Ortanique, Mineola
Satsuma: Early season	Clauselina, Okitsu, Owari, Satsuma
Tangerine	Tangerine, Tangelo hybrid
Clementine: Early season Mid season	Oroval, Fina, Orogrande Loretina, Oronules, Nova
Orange: Early season Mid season Late season	Navelina Navel Lane Late, Washington Navel, Sanguinella** Valencia Late, Navelate, Navel Powell Late
Lemon	Lunar or Cuatro Estaciones*, Fino, Verna, Eureka, Lisbon
Lime	Bear, Volkamericana
Grapefruit	Star ruby (red flesh), Red blush (pink flesh), Marsh (yellow flesh)

Notes: *This lemon flowers several times a year and therefore is perpetual-fruiting. There is also an old novelty variety named "the hand of Allah" because its fruit is like a distorted hand. But it's not very juicy nor very disease-resistant.
** This is a blood orange with red flesh.
For practical purposes:
Early season = End September to Christmas.
Mid season = January to March
Late season = April to June.

Hand of Allah

D. WHERE TO PLANT

The heights given in the table above are what we regard as safe. Undoubtedly there will be higher, south-facing locations on a southerly slope protected from cold winter winds and frost-free where the hardier citruses will grow. But recognise that you will be running a risk in bad winters.

Being evergreen citrus trees can be attractive in many situations, e.g. they can be grown as individual specimens inset in terraces, flower beds and lawns or planted as small groves or orchards in larger gardens, on steep banks. It is also possible to grow hedges of the denser-foliaged mandarin and both sweet and bitter orange bushes. When grafted on to a dwarf rooting stock, they can grow well in containers on apartment terraces, on roofs and in colder situations in a greenhouse or within the house.

If you have shallow soil or poor soil, citrus trees can be grown around the garden in tubs or raised beds. It would be perfectly possible to have a ten-tub fruit garden along the lines of the vegetable version (section 3.3) including a number of citrus trees.

E. BUYING TREES

Preferably buy from a garden centre or agricultural cooperative that has a good choice of trees. Some only have one type of orange with no indication whether it is early or late fruiting. Similarly with mandarins and lemons. If you are planning to plant trees in containers, check to see if they have trees on dwarf rooting stock. The least expensive will be young trees sold in narrow plastic sleeves, the next two or three-year-old trees in pots and the most expensive mature trees in large tubs.

In all cases select trees that look healthy with:
• Vigorous new growth.
• No signs of diseases or pests. Watch out for curling leaves with the burrows of the Mediterranean fruit fly, a yellowing of leaves due to chlorosis, white fluffy woolly aphids and small round black scales. (See section "L" below).
• No signs that the leaves are falling due to poor watering.
• No broken branches.
• A good embryo shape.
• No signs of branches dying back.
• Dwarf rootstocks if you want to plant in containers or raised beds.

With young trees check how long they have been grown in the tube bags. If grown there for some time, the roots may be developing a balanced root ball, but if recently packed for retail sale they may have all the roots squashed together. Either is acceptable, but you will need to plant them in different ways.

If buying a mature tree that has been cut back severely, check whether the tree has been specially grown for use as a specimen tree and has its best years to come or has been taken out of an orchard when almost at the end of its commercial life.

F. HOW TO PLANT YOUNG TREES TO GET THEM OFF TO A GOOD START

In theory citrus trees can be grown in any soils and with little water with careful husbandry. However, a great many citrus trees grown in gardens or newly planted orchards take a long time to establish themselves and yield good crops.

We therefore suggest that you plant as follows. Much of what we say has been learned the hard way.

Plant in the spring rather than the autumn
This will allow trees to acclimatise and put on growth before experiencing seriously cold weather.

Soil preparation
Citrus trees can grow in all sorts of soil, but if you have a clay or sandy soil it is worth improving the soil ahead of planting to make life easier later.

It is preferable to have a slightly sloping area for planting citrus trees to allow storm water to run away. Five degrees will probably be sufficient.

As for all fruit trees, citrus trees depend on a wide-spreading network of roots to collect moisture and nutrients. This will not happen if, for instance, you dig a planting hole in a heavy red clay soil only the diameter of the plastic sleeve bag that was around the root ball when you purchased the tree and then slide the root ball into the tight hole. Such soil soon dries like rock between waterings in the hot Spanish sun.

It is therefore recommended that you dig a hole 60 to 100cm wide and 40 to 50cm deep and then refill, mixing in one or two baskets of fully composted compost plus half a basket of fully composted manure. Do ensure that no uncomposted manure is used and that the soil, compost and manure is well mixed as putting raw manure against roots can cause fungal problems. As an alternative you can add five kilos of worm compost (humus de lombriz) that is now becoming widely available in garden centres. Allow the worked soil to settle for a week before you plant your trees.

Remember the health and eventual size of your trees will depend on their access to nutrients in competition with other trees and shrubs whether in an orchard or the flower garden. To reduce the competition, it's best to plant trees at least five metres apart and don't plant anything under citrus trees as their roots are mainly in the top 60 centimetres of soil.

Preparation of planting hole
As illustrated in the diagram opposite, the hole will depend on how you purchased your tree. Compared to many other fruit trees, citrus roots are relatively shallow. It is therefore important to plant your trees in soil that is sufficiently light to allow roots to spread unhindered.

POOR PLANTING

EFFECTIVE PLANTING

SOIL IN PLASTIC SLEEVE   UNIMPROVED POOR SOIL   IMPROVED SOIL

Planting your trees

As all citrus trees depend on a spreading root system, there are dangers in just plonking a tube or container-grown root ball directly into the ground. We suggest the following (see illustration):

> **a.** Dig a planting hole in the centre of your prepared ground. Firm the soil at the base and top it up and refirm until the soil level of the root ball to be planted will be proud of the surrounding soil.
>
> **b.** If you have purchased a dry rooted tree or a tree in a tube, first prepare a cone of firmed soil at the bottom of the hole (as illustrated) then open up the root ball around the cone. Then refill the hole with the earth you removed, firming it as you go.
>
> **c.** A three or four-year-old tree in a largish pot should already have a good root ball, so plant the root ball intact, ensuring the ball's level of soil sits proud of the surrounding ground. If not, take the tree out and repeat the process.
>
> **d.** Create a cone of soil around the trunk, ensuring that you do not bury the graft. This will ensure that water runs away from the trunk. You will find that most fruit trees for sale have been prepared by grafting a cutting of the variety you purchase on to the rootstock of another variety with either very vigorous or dwarf root systems.
>
> **e.** Create a circular watering trench one-and-a-quarter times the diameter of the root ball you have just planted and give the tree a good soaking. Check an hour later to see that it has not sunk and reversed the level of soil levels. If that occurs, rebuild the cone around the trunk and the watering trough.

Staking

In sheltered positions young trees will not require staking but in situations exposed to winter or summer winds stake all. Use a strong cane or stake appropriate to the size of tree and use soft ties that will not cut into or chaff the tender skin of the trunk.

Initial watering

Many young citrus trees die because of under and over-watering.

If you under-water, especially if you have not planted well, the soil around the root ball will shrink away from the roots and, if in unimproved clay soil, roots can be compressed by the contracting dry clay. It is important to recognise that the roots of citrus trees do not have numerous small roots along their surface.

Over-watering makes the roots and the base of the trunk susceptible to fungal attacks. So aim to keep the soil moist down to the deepest root. A deep watering once a week is better than a shallow watering every day or so. Falling leaves will soon tell you if you have it wrong.

Initial feeding

The roots of young trees can be easily burnt by strong, crystalline, inorganic, manufactured, basic fertilisers. Indeed, this is one of the major causes of the failure of young citrus trees as damage to young roots is generally irreversible.

If you have prepared your soil sufficiently, little feeding should be required. Any slowness of growth may be determined more by the lack of development of the root system or inadequate watering than a feeding problem. And, indeed, the biggest problem may be a large solid rock just a few centimetres under the roots and spreading sideways for a metre or so.

Trunk protection

The thin trunks of young trees can be scorched by blazing summer suns and freezing winter gales so protect them with plastic protection tubes or wraps.

Initial growth

Don't expect your new citrus trees to spring to life soon after you plant them. They won't until temperatures rise above 15 degrees C. This is why many citrus trees have a reasonable frost tolerance, as already illustrated. However, a warm winter spell followed by a few nights of frost can cause havoc if you gave the trees a nitrogen feed the previous autumn. The young growth thus stimulated is very vulnerable. It's better to be patient as explained above and below regarding the feeding and initial pruning of citrus trees. Don't prune young trees until the second or third spring (see section 4.2J).

Planting in containers

Plant in a good soil compost mix. We suggest a good proprietary fertile mix with sand or perlite mixed in to ensure good drainage without reducing the water holding properties of the organic matter. If you are an active gardener wishing to mix your own, try a 2.2.1 soil, compost heap compost, and sand mix.

G. PLANTING MATURE TREES

If you are impatient for fruit or need a large specimen for an architectural effect, you may find yourself paying a considerable sum for a large maturing tree. Also the tree will probably need a crane to lift it into position. So ensure that you prepare the planting area and hole well in advance, as explained for young trees but obviously on a larger scale. If you arrange for the garden centre where you purchased the tree to plant it for you, we suggest you ensure that the planting area is well-prepared, rather than just plonking the large root ball when lifted from its tub into a tight hole. The roots were possibly trimmed when the tree was lifted in a field in order to fit into the tub. They now need to lengthen rapidly to support the size of the large tree above the ground.

H. WATERING

One of the main causes of stunted or dead trees is the stress caused by poor watering practices.

Water to keep soil damp down to the root level. Recognise that like cacti citrus trees can dry out a long way before they suddenly wilt and cry out for water. Equally, dry trees will suffer more frost damage than trees in a damp soil should frost, like the winter of 2004/5, occur again. But obviously water more between March and September than during the cooler autumn and winter months unless you experience exceptionally hot dry periods and drying gales.

If you improved the soil before planting your trees, you will need to water less than if you have unimproved quick-draining, sandy soils. Also clay soil should be watered less as water-logged soils cause fungal problems. In commercial production a mature orange tree might be given up to 40 litres of water a day during the summer.

Always try to water at the natural drip line of the tree or just beyond to encourage root growth and keep excess water away from the trunk. If you over-water or rain water is allowed to stand round the trunks for some time, root fungal diseases can become a problem as the air/oxygen is pushed out of the soil (see section 4.11 for more details).

I. FEEDING

If you were growing commercially, you would probably give the trees supplementary feeds in January or February and then at six weekly intervals ceasing in August. This is to force the trees into rapid maturity and maximum yields. Grown in this way trees only have a useful commercial life of around 25 years, when the trees are replaced. We don't suggest this for the average domestic garden or small orchard. We give our trees two weak liquid feeds annually, first when flower buds appear and then when the fruit starts to appear.

A spring nitrogen-rich foliar feed as soon as new growth occurs can be beneficial especially after frost and for container-planted trees. Trees in pots will need a more regular nitrogen and potassium feed as the roots cannot travel far searching for nutrients. Use proprietary surface and foliar feeds especially recommended for citrus trees but use at double the recommended dilutions. Alternatively mix a couple of handfuls of worm compost into the surface soil each year.

Don't try to feed citrus trees with a surface mulch of manure as this tends to cause fungal attacks at the base of the trunk.

J. THE INITIAL PRUNING

Do the first pruning the second or third spring after you planted the trees. Restrict the pruning to removing a few upward-growing branches from the centre to start to let air and light in. If you plan to grow an architecturally attractive specimen rather than just an open lollipop, choose the two strongest branches at this stage to be the basis of the framework of branches that will be established over the next few years.

K. ONGOING ANNUAL PRUNINGS

There are several possible approaches to pruning your citrus trees.

Pruning with chisel

1. Treat the trees as ornamental trees and only trim out of shape, diseased, dead or broken branches. This will produce trees with a dense foliage and the number of flowers will be fantastic, but the fruit may tend to be smaller than if you had pruned harder. Also, when the sun does not get into the centre of the tree nor the air circulates freely inside the foliage, trees are more vulnerable to disease and pest problems.

Thinning centres

2. You can prune as in number "1" and then open up the centre by removing some upward-growing and crossing branches in the centre and do no more. This will help control pests and diseases.

3. You can do as in "2", plus pruning out the minor centre branch at the end of each branch after flowering to reduce the number of fruit that will form while probably increasing their potential sizes. The size achieved will depend on your approach to watering and feeding.

4. You could do as in "1" or "2" and then trim

the outside of the tree immediately after harvesting and during the growing season as if it were a lightly trimmed cypress hedge. This is a good way with ornamental boundary or internal hedges. Naturally this will reduce the number of fruit.

Thinning smaller branches

5. Just trim the outside leaving the middle alone. This is now done on some commercial orange farms that prune after harvesting with trimmers attached to tractors to reduce costs. This works if the need is for as many juicing oranges as possible, but they are likely to be small.

6. Prune for optimum fruit size by starting to shape a tree systematically from its third year of growth. In that year remove all the branches on the trunk down to two or three which will become the main branches. Then continue along these lines for two or three further years so that the framework of branches develops as illustrated below.

EVOLUTION OF STRUCTURE OF MAIN BRANCHES
BY SYSTEMATIC ARCHITECTUAL PRUNING
Age of orange tree-years

| 2/3 | 3 | 4 | 6 | 8 |

Age of Orange Tree - Years

7. In all cases prune off growth that develops beneath the graft.

8. In all cases but "4" decide whether you want the tree to appear like a bush with growth to the ground or trim off the lower branches to whatever trunk size trunk height you want.

9. Lemons tend to grow more vigorously than other citrus trees and are therefore best pruned differently unless you are happy with eventually having a large tree in height and width yielding thousands of lemons a year but requiring harvesting from a ladder. For the average garden we suggest you prune back some of the vigorously growing branches on young trees and remove all crossing branches. Before many years you will have an attractive two-metre high tree yielding plenty of lemons within easy reach.

10. If your trees are damaged by the frost, leave until new growth appears and then cut out any seriously damaged or dead growth. If you cut back too early, the cut branches will probably die back further. Don't be in too much of a hurry to write off an apparently dead tree. It may not sprout back to life for a few months. When it does, a sprayed foliar feed rich in nitrogen will accelerate the recovery of the foliage and stimulate new growth. After the worst frosts for 50 years in 2004 we sprayed our trees, the lemon being the worst affected, with a home-made nettle spray.

11. If you take over a garden with uncared-for trees, they will benefit from a remedial pruning in the first March that you own the property. First, cut out any obviously dead, dying, damaged and diseased growth. Treat the surface of major cuts with a black pruning sealer paint. If this leaves very few leaves, cut back the main skeleton of branches to a balanced shape. Give the tree a root and foliar nitrogen feed and water regularly. In many cases new growth will develop within a few weeks but it may be months.

12. Guidelines for how much vegetation to remove are as follows:

> **A light prune:** 10 per cent
> **Normal annual prunings:** 20 per cent
> **Hard pruning after frost damage:** 30 per cent
> **Very heavy remedial pruning of old unkempt trees:** 50 per cent

13. Much of what is said above also relates to trees in containers, although in most cases you will probably opt for styles "1", "2" or "4".

L. COPING WITH COMMON PROBLEMS

The most common problems you may encounter are:

- Excessive leaf fall can be caused by too little watering, need for a nitrogen feed, pests or a touch of frost.
- Sunburn of the trunk can be prevented by wrapping the trunk of young trees with a trunk protector tube or by painting the trunk with a white wash. Special washes may be available at your local agricultural cooperative. As the tree grows, low branches will provide protective shade. Should young trunks be burnt, the bark will harden and split allowing fungal diseases to enter.
- Fruit drop of small fruit after flowering is normal, but if it continues as the fruit swells you may be watering too little or have fed the tree too much nitrogen and it is producing leaves in preference to fruit. Spraying in the summer with strong insecti-

cides can also cause the problem (see sections 5.1 and 5.7).

• Fruit splitting can occur if you experience a cycle of dramatic changes in weather conditions or you suddenly water a distressed tree for the first time for weeks.

• Root rot can be caused by excessive moisture and the use of too much fertiliser, especially strong inorganic chemical fertilisers, so take care.

• The main insect problems likely to be experienced are leaf miners, fruit flies, aphids, mealy bugs, red spider mite, trips, sooty leaves and scale. Some possible preventive actions and controls are provided in section 5.7.

We prefer to use ecological/organic solutions for health reasons, even if not achieving total control. If you prefer to use manufactured inorganic sprays, do read and follow the instructions carefully. Wear protective clothing - face mask, rubber gloves and boots - when spraying, and store the containers in a safe, airy place.

In general, pests will disfigure a tree and reduce its fruit crops but will rarely kill the tree. We note that some commercial producers are now reducing their insecticide spraying to reduce costs as they make little profit from their trees. However, this is not a sensible approach within your garden where the first priority is for citrus trees to look good.

M. HARVESTING AND STORAGE

We prefer to pick citrus fruit when ripe and least acidic. A juicy sweet, pre-Christmas tangerine or a late end-of-season navel orange straight off the tree is very different to many fruits on sale commercially. This is mainly because the latter were picked unripe, even green in early season.

Often we are asked: "Why are my home-grown oranges less shiny and with less colour than those in the supermarket?" There are good reasons. If you look at your tree, you will find that the fruit in full sun are possibly more coloured than those in shade or semi-shade. You may have suffered some weather damage, particularly from hail. Also you have not put your fruit through a colouring bath to make them a common colour and mask out blemishes or through a wax bath to polish them, as occurs in packing stations.

Fruit picked before fully ripe will store in trays in a cool dark place for a month or so, particularly lemons. Short-term supplies can be kept in the fridge. But the best is a fruit bowl topped up every day or so with ripe fruit from your trees.

See also section 4.16.

4.3 STONE FRUITS

A. MAIN USES AND BENEFITS

All stone fruits are grown to eat from the tree with the exception of avocados, which are normally picked unripe and ripened as required, and olives, which are pickled or pressed for oil. Many of the fruits can also be cooked, bottled and made into jams.

B. TYPES OF FRUIT TREE POSSIBLE

TYPE OF FRUIT TREE English, Spanish and botanical names	Form	TBT	THT	TPT
APRICOT Albaricoquero *Armeniaca bulgaris*	Tree	April/May	May/June	W
AVOCADO Aguacate *Persia gratisoima*	Tree/ Bush	Jan/Mar	Oct/June	Spr
JAJUBE Azufaifo *Ziziphus jujaba*	Tree	April/May	Sep/Oct	W
CHERRY Cerezo Prunus avium	Tree	Mar/Apr	May/June	W
CUSTARD APPLE Chirimoyo Chirimoya anona	Tree	Mar/April	Aug/Oct	W
DATE PALM Palmera *Phoenix dactylifera*	Tree	June/Aug	Sep/Oct	W
LYCHEE Lichi *Lichi chinensis*	Tree	April/May	July/Sep	W
MANGO Mango *Mangifera indica*	Bush/ Tree	April/June	Aug/Sep	Spr
MEDLAR Níspero europeo **Mespilus germanica**	Tree	April/May	Sep/Oct	W
NECTARINE Nectarina *Prunus persica*	Tree	April/May	May/July	W
NÍSPERO/LOQUAT Níspero de Japón/dulce *Eriobotryra japonica*	Tree	Oct/Nov	April/May	Spr

Typical planting heights above sea level (metres)					PR	DR	FR
< 200	< 400	< 800	< 1200	> 1200			
*	*				M	H	H
*	*				H	M	M
*	*				M	M	H
*	*	*	*		H	M	H
*	*				H	M	M
*	*	*			M	H	H
*	*	*	*	*	M	L/M	M/H
*	*				H	M	L
	*	*	*		M	M	M
*	*				M	M	H
*	*				M	M/H	M

TYPE OF FRUIT TREE English, Spanish and botanical names	Form	TBT	THT	TPT
OLIVE Olivo *Olea europea*	Tree	March/April	Nov/Feb	W
PARAGUAYA Paraguaya *Prunus paraguaya*	Tree	April/May	July/Aug	W
PEACH Melocotonero *Prunus perica*	Tree	April/May	June/Sep	W
PLUM Ciruelo **Prunus sativa**	Tree	Mar/Apr	Jun/July	W
SLOE Endrino *Prunus spinosa*	Bush/ Tree	April/May	Aug/Sept	W

Notes:
TBT = Typical blossom time. **THT** = Typical harvest time.
TPT = Typical pruning time. **W** = Winter and **Spr** = Spring.
PR = Pest resistance. **DR** = Drought resistance. **FR** = Frost resistance.
H = High. **M** = Medium. **L** = Low.

Avocados

Avocado flowers

Dates

Jajube

Apricots

74

Typical planting heights above sea level (metres)					PR	DR	FR
 200	 400	 800	 1200	> 1200			
*	*	*	*		M	H	H
*					M	M	L
*	*	*			M	M	H
*	*	*	*	*	M	M	H
	*	*	*		H	H	H

Lichee

Nispero

Peach

Mango

Nactarine

Sloes

Plums

75

C. CHOICE OF VARIETIES

A choice of varieties of apricot, avocado, cherry, loquat, olive, peach and plum trees should be available in your local nursery or agricultural cooperative. Some will be early-flowering and fruiting varieties and others late varieties. You can plant both for continuity or just the latter to avoid frosts. Take their advice as to which grow best in your area.

If you are only planting one or two olive trees we suggest you select varieties such as *manzanilla* or *cacereña*, which are among the best for pickling. Many varieties are used for the production of good olive oil.

D. WHERE TO PLANT

All can be grown as specimen trees within the garden or in orchards. Peaches and nectarines are often trained on south-facing walls in the form of a fan. Before deciding which fruit trees to buy it is important to note the indication of frost resistance in the table above.

As discussed in section 5.6, the frost-sensitive, semi-tropical paraguaya, avocado, and tropical mango will need to be grown in sheltered frost-free sunny situations. This means essentially along the coastal plain and the further south the better. Many locations in the Canary Islands are ideal.

E. HOW TO PLANT AND GET OFF TO A GOOD START

If you are not in a heavy frost or snow area, stone fruit trees can be planted from October until March - later if container-grown. If you do suffer cold winters, delay your plantings until March.

All stone fruit trees benefit from being planted in earth previously enriched by digging well-rotted compost/manure to improve the water retention and fertility of the soil. See section 4.2F for guidelines on the preparation of soils and planting holes and the process of planting and staking.

F. WATERING AND FEEDING

All young trees require regular watering until their deep roots are established, normally after three or four years. Beyond that, water just before flowering and when the fruit is swelling and ripening if there is no rain. Fruit trees in gardens do not normally require continuous feeding but, if your trees fail to have much blossom or few fruits stay on until harvesting, give them a feed in early spring. The best feed is a mulch of well-rotted compost/manure, a general granular slow-release fertiliser high in potash/potassium, or five kilos of worm compost spread around the drip line of the tree. If you use a fertiliser high in nitrogen, it will stimulate the growth of new branches and leaves rather than the development of flowers and fruit.

A combined insect control and foliar feeding is often given to improve yields and the general health of trees and emergent fruits. Organically, a combined nettle, sulphur, neem spray could be used.

G. COPING WITH COMMON PESTS AND DISEASES

The most common insect problem with stone fruit trees is the Mediterranean fruit fly. The best thing is to spray pre and post-flowering with a neem oil/water emulsion, potassium soap solution or a proprietary light oil spray. It also helps to fix grease/glue bands around the trunks during the winter and spring. Traps hung on the branches can also be helpful at this time and later fallen fruit should be cleaned up and not put on the compost heap. These and other problems such as leaf curl are discussed in section 5.7.

H. RECOMMENDED PRUNINGS

See section 4.13.

HARVESTING AND STORAGE

Fruit for eating is the most delicious when picked fully ripe off the tree the day you plan to eat it. Naturally, fruit can be picked unripe and allowed to ripen in a fruit bowl, but it will never be as good as fresh from the tree. Excess fruit can be bottled, frozen and made into jams or chutneys. Fruit for these purposes is best picked ripe but not over-ripe.

If you have a vegetable/fruit dryer it is also possible to produce your own dried apricots and prunes (dried plums). See section 4.16.

Avocados are normally picked hard and kept in boxes in a cool cellar and used as they ripen. Ripening can be accelerated by wrapping each fruit in newspaper and placing in a dark drawer or cupboard. The ripening can be further accelerated by wrapping up a banana skin with the avocado.

Olives for pickling are best picked while still firm and by hand. Our recipe is given below.

The best virgin olive oil will be obtained by processing fully ripe fruit that have been hand-picked, not been attacked by the olive fly or other pathogens and not allowed to stand around and start to ferment before processing.

A lower quality with a less fresh taste and higher acidity will be achieved from unripe, diseased, partially fermented fruit and fruit bruised by knocking them off the trees with a cane.

The pressing of olives to produce olive oil requires approximately five to six kilos of olives per litre of oil. If you have a large harvest you can normally arrange for these to be pressed at an olive mill owned by the local agricultural cooperative. There are normally minimum requirements for processing your olives separately. Smaller quantities can be pressed in conjunction with the crops of a Spanish neighbour.

See also section 4.17.

OUR BASIC RECIPE FOR THE HOME PREPARATION OF OLIVES

1. Pick your olives when ripe. Discard those badly bruised or with signs of insect damage. Best to pick them directly off the trees.
2. Soak in a bucket of water (preferably non-chlorinated) for four to five weeks, changing the water every two to three days. This removes most of the bitter taste that freshly harvested olives have.
3. Prepare a brine. Dissolve salt in cold water by stirring vigorously. Every so often put a fresh egg in its shell in the brine. When it just floats to the top it is the correct strength.
4. Collect some thyme and fill jars or a large earthenware container with alternate layers of olives and a twig of thyme.
5. Fill the jars with brine and float two or three carob leaves on the surface. This is good for preventing mould. You can process the green and black olives separately or together.
6. Seal the jars or cover the earthenware container with a sheet of plastic and store in a cellar for three months before starting to use.
A speedier processing can be achieved by squashing the olives lightly with a wooden mallet or slitting them with a knife before putting in brine.
7. When ready, open a jar. Drain off the brine. Fill the jar with fresh water twice to rinse off excess salt and then place in an olive jar or bowl and cover with olive oil to which a few rosemary twigs have been added and a garlic clove if to your taste. Leave a couple of days and they are ready for tapas or a salad.
 · Alternative finishes include adding a little hot red pepper, anis or a salted anchovy to the olive oil.
 · Alternative starting recipes include adding carrot, onion, garlic, chilli pepper, a slice of lemon or orange, a bay leaf, fennel seeds, and a little cider vinegar to the starter brine in the jars. Try your own experiments. Even one tree can produce a large harvest.
 · If there is a little mould on the carob leaves and surface, when you open the olives just discard it.
 · Alternatively you can process some fully ripe, even shrivelled, black olives by packing them in a large jar or barrel between layers of dry salt. We love the late-harvested, frosted Aragón olives produced that way.

4.4 PIP AND SEED FRUITS (excluding soft fruits): MAIN USES AND BENEFITS

All the pip and seed fruits listed can be eaten without cooking when ripe with the exception of quince and crab apples which are normally converted into jelly. All fruits are high in vitamins. The banana is particularly high in potassium and therefore loved by walkers and tennis players to prevent cramp. The juice of the pomegranate is useful as a meat tenderiser. Many of the fruits can be incorporated in cooked meat and fish dishes, desserts and jams.

TYPES OF FRUIT TREE POSSIBLE

The large number of pip fruits that can be grown in Spain are described in the following table.

TYPE OF FRUIT TREE English, Spanish and botanical names	Form	TBT	THT	TPT
APPLE Manzano *Malus communis*	Tree	March/Apr	Aug/Oct	W
BANANA* Platanera *Musa paradisiaca*	Tree	Apr/July	Sept/Mar	W
CRAB APPLE Manzano silvestre *Malus floribunda*	Tree	Mar/Apr	Aug/Oct	W
ELDERBERRY Baya del sauco *Sambucus canadensis*	Tree	May/Jun	Aug	W
FIG Higuera *Ficus Carica*	Tree	* *	Aug/Oct	W
GUAVA Guayaba *Psidium guajava*	Tree	Apr/May	July/Aug	W
AZEROLE Azerolo *Crataegus azarolus*	Tree	April	Aug/Sep	W
LYCHEE Lichi *Litchi chinensis*	Tree	April/May	July/Sep	W
MULBERRY Morera *Morus negra*	Tree	April/May	Jun/July	W
PAPAYA Papaya *Carica papaya*	Tree	Mar/June	Jun/Nov	W
PEAR Peral *Pyrus communis*	Tree	March/Apr	Aug/Oct	W

Typical planting heights above sea level (metres)					PR	DR	FR
< 200	< 400	< 800	< 1200	> 1200			
*	*	*	*	*	M	M	H
*	*				M	M	L
*	*	*	*	*	M	M	H
	*	*	*		H	L	H
*	*	*			M	H	H
*					M	M	L
*	*				M	M	H
					M	M	H
*	*	*			H	L	L
*	*	*	*	*	M	M	H
*	*	*			M	M	H

TYPE OF FRUIT TREE English, Spanish and botanical names	Form	TBT	THT	TPT
PRICKLY PEAR CACTUS Higo chumbo *Opuntia ficus indica*	Tree/ Bush	May/July	Aug/Sep	W
POMEGRANATE Granado *Punica granatum*	Tree	May	Oct/Feb	W
QUINCE Membrillero *Cydona oblonga*	Tree	Apr/May	Sep/Oct	W
STRAWBERRY TREE Madroño *Arbutus unedo*	Tree	Oct/Dec	Oct/Jan ***	-

Notes

TBT = Typical blossom time. **THT** = Typical harvest time. **TPT** = Typical pruning time. **W** = Winter. **PR** = Pest resistance. **DR** = Drought resistance. **FR** = Frost restance. **H** = High. **M** = Medium. **L** = Low.

* The banana plant is normally referred to as a tree although it is in fact a large perennial herb. ** Flowers not visible as they are in fact enclosed within the forming fruit.*** The fruit takes 12 months to develop and ripen and is therefore on the tree at the same time as the next year's flowers.

Apples

Banana

Elderberry

Fig

Typical planting heights above sea level (metres)					PR	DR	FR
 200	 400	 800	 1200	> 1200			
*	*	*			H	H	M/H
*	*	*			H	M	H
*	*	*	*		M	H	H
*	*	*			M	M	H

Kaki

Pears

Pomegranate

Prickly Pear

Quince

83

C. CHOICE OF VARIETIES

A choice of varieties of apple, figs and pears are likely to be available in your local garden centres and agricultural cooperative. Take their advice as to which grow best in your area and check whether the varieties are self-fertile or diploid, in which case you will need to plant another variety nearby to achieve cross pollination. If you have space, plant a number of varieties that are ready to harvest at different times. For instance there is a breva fig that fruits twice. Its first crop of black fruit can be harvested in late spring and its second in mid-summer, the same time as other varieties of figs.

D. WHERE TO PLANT

Apple, crab apple, jajube, mulberry, pear, persimmon, pomegranate, prickly pear, quince and strawberry trees can be grown in any of the situations described in Part Three. Being temperate they can also be grown at higher altitudes than citrus trees.

Bananas, guavas, lichees and papayas are tropical and therefore need to be grown at low altitudes in warm frost-free situations. A prickly pear hedge is hard to beat to keep people and animals out - it also acts as a good fire break.

HOW TO PLANT. See section 4.2F.

WATERING AND FEEDING. See sections 4.3F, 4.11 and 5.3.

COPING WITH COMMON PESTS AND DISEASES. See section 5.7.

RECOMMENDED PRUNINGS. See section 4.13.

Unpruned fig tree

Pruned fig tree

I. HARVESTING, STORING AND PROCESSING

As with all fruit, pip fruits are most enjoyable when picked ripe off the tree. However, many store reasonably well if picked unripe, laid on a cool floor or shelves for a few weeks before being trayed or boxed with each fruit wrapped in paper or with clean straw between and stored in a cool, dark, dry place. Hands of bananas are often cut when green or just turning yellow and hung up in a cool, dark place, fruit being removed for ripening in a fruit bowl as required.

Many make good jams and quince *(membrillo)* jelly is popular with cheese. Quinces are best kept for a few weeks after harvesting before being processed into jelly.

Try drying your own figs and apple slices in a tray drier, as illustrated in section 4.3I.

Heavy-grade gloves are necessary when harvesting prickly pears. The worst spikes can be first removed by running a short piece of wood over the entire surface of the fruit. The fruit is best cut in half and the flesh scooped out into a bowl ready for eating, making into jam or a liquor. See also section 4.17.

4.5 NUTS

A. MAIN USES AND BENEFITS

Nuts are generally recognised as a valuable source of energy, protein, mono-saturated fats, folic acid, potassium, magnesium, zinc and other trace elements. Thus, a small bowl of nuts in their shells, cracked as required and eaten slowly, is a more beneficial snack than a packet of roasted or fried salted nuts.

Nuts can be eaten when out walking - we always have a few almonds and walnuts in our rucksacks - as a snack or tapas, in salads and cooked dishes and as ingredients in desserts and cakes.

Once established, they need little care except for an annual pruning and spray against insects. On taller trees, such as walnut and chestnut, this becomes impossible if allowed to grow to their full natural heights. When mature they are a good source of summer shade.

There are some tasty meat and fish dishes based on nuts, such as trout and rabbit, eels or angler fish stewed in an almond/garlic sauce. Nuts, especially walnuts, are a useful addition to salads. Pine kernels can be added to many cooked dishes and are an important centre of meat balls prepared for paellas.

B. TYPES OF NUT POSSIBLE

The following types of nut are regularly grown in gardens in Spain. Their frost hardiness makes them particularly attractive for growing from the shore line to way up in the mountains. The first choice for most is an almond tree, not only for its nuts but for the first blossom of the year (jointly with flowering acacias).

English, Spanish and botanical names	Relative		Typical flowering times**	Typical harvest times**	Typical heights above sea level (metres)
	Height	Width			
ALMOND Almendra *Prunus amygdalus*	M	M/H	Jan/Feb	Aug	< 600
CAROB* Algarroba *Ceratonia*	M/H	M/H	Feb	Aug/Oct	< 600
CHESTNUT Castaña *Castanea sativa*	H	M/H	Apr/May	Oct	300 to 1000
HAZEL Avellana *Corylus avellano*	M/L	M/L	Apr/May	Oct/Nov	300 to 800
MACADAMIA Macadamia *Proteacea macademia*	M	M	Apr/May	Sept/Oct	< 200
PECAN Pacana *Carya peca*	M/H	H	Apr/May	Sept/Nov	100 to 800
PINE KERNEL Piñón *Pinus pinea*	M	H	Mar/Apr	Oct/Nov	All
PISTACHIO Pistacho *Pistacia vera*	M	M	Apr/May	Sept/Oct	100 to 600
WALNUT Nuez *Juglans regia*	H	H	Apr/May	Sept/Nov	200 to 1000

Notes

PR = Pest resistance. **DR** = Drought resistance. **H**= High, **M** = Medium, **L**= Low.

* Carob, not strictly a nut, is included here for convenience.

** Can vary by a few weeks depending on height and latitude of garden.

NB: Peanuts are grown as a root vegetable and dealt with in section 4.9. A large crop will need about the same square metres as a nut tree on a vegetable plot, but useful quantities can be grown in large flower pots on the terrace.

PR	DR	FR
H	M/H	H
H	H	H
M	M	H
H	M	M/H
H	M	L
M	H	H
H	H	H
H	M	M/H
M	H	H

Almonds

Carob

Walnuts

Chestnuts

C. CHOICE OF VARIETIES

There are several varieties of almonds. Some have pink and others white blossom, some elongated nuts and others more rounded. The obvious thing is to buy the variety of almond that has been traditionally grown in your area. You will probably only find one variety of other types of fruit.

D. WHERE TO PLANT

All grow to sizeable trees and therefore need to be given ample room as stand-alone specimen trees or within small mixed copses or orchards. They can be planted towards the boundary of a property to screen unsightly buildings and the hazelnut trees can be trained as a thick hedge, although losing their leaves in the winter. The roots of mature trees are likely to spread well beyond the outer foliage and drip line of the trees to act as guy ropes to support the tree as well as searching for moisture, so do not plant too near to house and boundary walls. Also since the trees often produce a network of shallow roots this may constrain what you can plant nearby. For this reason they are often planted in the centre of lawns.

E. HOW TO PLANT

Prepare the soil as follows.
1. If the soil is rock-hard, soak well before starting to dig.
2. Double-dig a two-metre-diameter area down to 60 to 80 centimetres and work in three or four large buckets of well-rotted compost/manure.
3. Dig a central planting hole, knock in a support stake, fill the hole with water and let the water drain away.
4. Plant the tree spreading the roots as wide and equally spaced as possible and tying the trunk to the stake for support.
5. Fill in the hole, firming the soil as you proceed.
If you are planting a tall sapling especially one sold dry-rooted with a limited root ball, fix four guy ropes to the top of the support post spaced equally around the tree.

F. WATERING AND FEEDING

Young trees will need regular watering until established.
Mature trees will need watering in periods of long drought for maximum health and crops.
Buried irrigation systems are excellent for orchards of mature trees to ensure the roots are wet and to reduce evaporation.
It is beneficial to enrich the soil with well-rotted compost/manure before planting.
Normally nut trees are grown in gardens without being fertilised so as to control the size of the trees. However, if you can accommodate full-sized mature trees, fertilise away from the trunk around the drip line where rain will wash the nutrients down to the concentration of roots. The use of a thin layer of rotted compost or manure can be sufficient.

If you use manufactured biological or chemical fertilisers, purchase one high in potash to stimulate flowers and nuts. Fertilise late winter.

G. COPING WITH COMMON PESTS AND DISEASES

The main problems with nut trees are:

Fungal diseases, especially on old trees. Best preventive action is not to water close to the trunks and to prune out any branches that show signs of fungal growths.

Codling moths which lay eggs in the forming nuts. When they hatch, the grubs feed on the nut kernels and infested nuts can affect others in storage. Grease bands on young trees give some protection and a neem spray in the autumn after harvesting and before and after flowering is useful. Also dry and sort nuts before storing.

Wood-boring beetles. Watch for dying branches and immediately check whether bore holes can be seen. Remove dying branches as soon as possible. A heavy infestation will result in a tree dying and requiring felling before it is dangerous.

See section 5.7 for more details.

H. RECOMMENDED PRUNINGS

Nut trees generally only require pruning when young to encourage a balanced shape. Later cut out any diseased branches or any broken in gales. Also prune off any suckers and low-growing young branches below the developing crown of main branches. See section 4.12 for more details.

I. HARVESTING AND STORAGE

The typical times of harvesting are indicated in the table above. Harvest when nuts start to fall. Pick by hand on short trees and knock off with a cane on taller trees, unless you have the nerve to climb into the upper reaches suitably safety-harnessed and employing a long cane.

Leave on very tall trees until they fall naturally, but harvest daily from the ground to minimise the entry of insects and the nuts becoming damp and starting to rot.

Dry the nuts in the sun and separate any outer casings before storing in hessian or woven plastic sacks or boxes in a cool, dry cellar or garage where they can keep for a couple of years if not attacked by weevils. If you have an attack, place a bowl of sodium metabisulphite near the nuts.

It's best to store nuts in their shells until required as shelled nuts can soon lose their freshness even in sealed containers.

See also section 4.16.

4.6 TROPICAL SPECIALITIES

A. RECOGNISE THE RISKS FROM DAY ONE

Most gardeners living in the Canary Islands and in the sheltered low valleys of the Costa del Sol and Costa Tropical will have the ideal climate for growing tropical fruits. However, we have seen tropical fruits grown right up the Mediterranean coastal plain and in sheltered inland valley situations. But, the further north you go, the more essential it is to grow them in south-facing plots, sheltered on three sides from winds and with very little or preferably no chance of frosts.

The March frosts of 2005 highlighted the latter point very clearly. Avocado plantations even near the Andalusia coast were affected and an enviable sheltered garden near Gandia in Valencia lost, for the first time in many years, some of its collection of lychee, papaya, banana, avocado and mango trees.

If you are situated in an inland valley, recognise the risks from day one. On south-facing slopes it is possible to grow frost-sensitive fruit provided you shelter the trees as described above and cover them with fleece, bubble wrap and green wind-proof material from the middle of November until the end of March. This saved our young avocado but we lost a mango tree from which the previous summer we had harvested 25 juicy fruit - not hard like many in the supermarkets. But that experience was so good we immediately planted a replacement, though knowing that we might have to wait five years for a similar crop.

B. WHAT IS POSSIBLE

With care, a little luck and an adventuresome spirit the following are possible: avocados, bananas, lychees, mangoes, papayas and pineapples.

They are all described in the previous sections with the exception of the pineapple. These can be cultivated by cutting the head off a purchased pineapple, removing the outer ring of dry petals, drying in the sun for a few days, spraying the cut/dry base with a fungicide and rooting powder and then planting shallowly in a gritty, open but rich, compost in flower pots placed in a greenhouse, cold frame or on a sunny sheltered area. With luck roots will start to develop within a few weeks and a new plant start to develop. Keep damp and feed monthly with a nitrogen feed until a healthy, obviously growing plant is developing. After a year switch over to a high potassium feed to stimulate the development of a flower and fruit.

If you are definitely not in a frost belt, the plants can be planted out in a flower bed, terrace plot or on the vegetable plot.

If you want to be adventurous and won't be put off by a few early failures, also have a go at growing papaya or star fruits from the seeds inside a ripe purchased fruit. Bananas can also be grown from seed and indeed the seed catalogue of Chiltern seeds (www.chilternseeds.com) normally lists 10 or 12 varieties from different locations world-wide including species that are relatively frost-hardy.

Banana

Papaya

If you have a large greenhouse or conservatory, a range of tropical fruits can be grown Kew-Gardens-style.

Whether planted in the garden, in pots or in a greenhouse all will need a rich water-retaining but free-draining soil and the continuous availability of water for irrigation. Some, like the banana, will require copious watering. And banana skins and chopped up leaves are the natural way of mulching banana trees to recycle the potassium content to stimulate more flowers and fruits.

Papaya

Pineapple

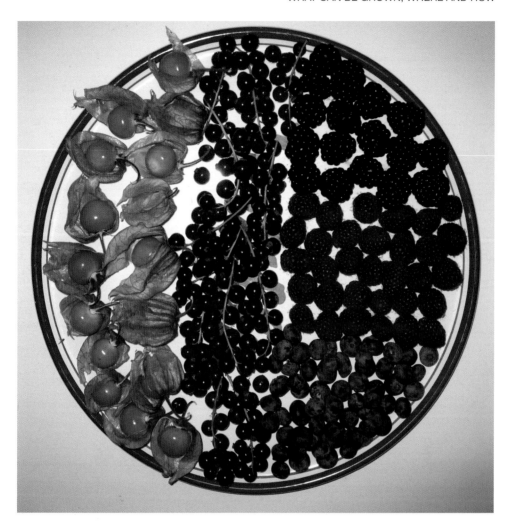

4.7 SOFT FRUITS

MAIN USES AND BENEFITS

Soft fruits are wonderful fresh, in tarts, cheesecakes or summer puddings. They are considered to be good sources of vitamins but can be acidic if eaten unripe. Alpine strawberries can be used as a ground-cover living mulch in perennial/shrub beds or to cover a shaded bank.

A. TYPES OF FRUIT POSSIBLE

The following are all possible especially if you garden more than 400 metres above sea level or in a northerly region.

PLANT NAME English, Spanish and botanical names	THT	Space required I, M, H	Ease of growing E, WC, D
BLACKBERRY Zarzamora *Rubus fruticosus*	Jun/Sep	M	WC
BLACKCURRANT Grosella negra *Ribes nigrum*	May	L	WC
BLUEBERRY Arándano *Vaccinium*	Jun/Sep	L	WC
CAPE GOOSEBERRY (1) Physalis *Physalis peruviana*	Aug/Sep	L	WC
GOOSEBERRY Uva espina, Grosella espinosa *Ribes grossularia*	May/Jun	L	D
LOGANBERRY Frambuesa norteamericana *Rubus logan*	Jun/Oct	M	D
RASPBERRY Frambuesa *Rubus idaeus*	May/Nov	M/H	WC
REDCURRANT Grosella roja *Ribes rubrum*	Apr/May	L	WC
RHUBARB Ruibarbo *Rheum x hybridum*	May/Jun	L	D
STRAWBERRY (cultivated) Fresón *Fragaria aranassa*	Feb/Oct	Barrel low M/H for larger crops	E
ALPINE STRAWBERRY Fresa *Fragaria vesca*	Mar/Sep	M	E

Typical planting heights (metres)				PR	DR	FR
< 200	< 400	< 800	> 800			
•	•	•	•	H	M	H
•	•	•	•	M	L	H
		•	•	M	M	H
•	•			M	M	L
		•	•	M	L	H
	•	•	•	H	L	H
	•	•	•	H	L	H
•	•	•	•	M	L	H
	•	•	•	L	L	M
•	•	•	•	M	M	H
	•	•	•	H	M	H

PLANT NAME English, Spanish and botanical names	THT	Heading requiered I, M, H	Ease of growing E, WC, D
TAYBERRY Tayberry *Rubus tay*	Jun/Oct	M	D

Notes:
THT = Typical harvest time in months.
Minimum space required to achieve worthwhile harvests:
L = Low (less than 1sqm {one square metre}); **M** = Medium (less than 5sqm); **H** = High (more than 10sqm).
Ease of growing: **E** = Easy; **WC** = With care; **D**= Difficult.
Typical growing heights above sea level.
PR = Pest and disease resistance: **H** = High; **M** = Moderate; **L**= Low.
DR = Drought resistance: H=High; M = Moderate; L= Low.
(1) Also known as ground cherry and goldenberry.

Raspberries

Cape gooseberry

Strawberries

Typical planting heights (metres)				PR	DR	FR
 200	 400	 800	> 800			
•	•	•	•	H	L	H

B. CHOICE OF PLANTS

Those who grew soft fruits before coming to Spain will find the availability of plants and choice of varieties limited. We suggest you purchase plants whenever you see the opportunity at a realistic price. If they seem expensive, buy a few plants or one or two bushes and immediately propagate by taking cuttings and potting up or planting in a corner of the garden. Strawberries can be expanded and replaced every three years by cutting off and planting young runners.

Various varieties of strawberries including the small wild/Alpine strawberries can be relatively easily grown from seed sown in pots in the spring.

Rhubarb you will probably only find in the north of Spain.

C. WHERE TO PLANT

Plant in sunny or semi-shaded situations. The options include:

1. Growing strawberries on a terrace in earthenware, plastic or wooden strawberry barrels which have holes for the plants or in window boxes.
2. Alpine strawberries make an excellent weed-inhibiting undergrowth for a mixed shrub/perennial bed. They also inhibit water evaporation and the state of the plants in the summer months give an early warning of when a bed is drying out and requires watering.
3. A dedicated soft fruit bed in a sunny corner of the flower or vegetable garden or orchard.
4. Rambling blackberries, loganberries or tayberries grown on walls or fences.
5. Down the gap between lines of fruit trees in an orchard.
6. Currant bushes worked into a shrub bed.
7. Cape gooseberries grown as a line of tomatoes or in one or two containers.
8. Blueberries in the semi-shade of trees and within or on the edge of an orchard.
9. Rhubarb needs to be planted in a damp, semi-shaded place and given shelter from hot suns. It is not easy to establish in Spain. The greatest problem is that, since even the roots are fleshy and succulent, it attracts slugs and snails from metres around, especially in hot weather. Galicia and the north would have a good climate for it.

D. HOW TO PLANT

All soft fruits benefit from a rich, moisture-retaining, slightly acid but not water-logged soil. So dig in plenty of well-rotted compost and/or manure. Use bags of organic fertiliser or peat substitute if you have none available.

Strawberries are best planted between September and October and December when the weather has cooled off but is still warm enough to stimulate root growth and strong crowns. To retain moisture, prevent shallow roots from drying out and prevent water-logging, it is preferable to plant strawberries through holes in black plastic on the side slopes of a shallow ridge or on a raised bed.

Also plant raspberries on a low ridge and mulch well initially with well-rotted or sacked organic compost. We then top up several times a year with comfrey leaves and grass cuttings from neighbours' lawns on which no chemical treatments have been used. Support the canes on wires strung between strong posts. Plant, mulch and train blackberry, tayberry and loganberry vines similarly.

Currant, blueberry and gooseberry plants can be planted on the flat with similar mulching. To reduce the amount of space required, currants and gooseberry plants can be pruned and trained as cordons.

Cape gooseberries are an oddity in that they are grown as if they are tomatoes - they are grown from seed and need staking as they grow about a metre high. They take up little space so can be grown as a line of vegetables anywhere in the garden in one or two tubs on an apartment terrace.

They have an attractive tart taste and can be eaten raw or made into jam. When the fruits form, they are enclosed in shell-like calyces. When the latter dries out, the fruit is ready for harvesting. When the plants die back in the autumn, remove all the roots as they are evasive. It is possible to treat the plants as perennials by potting up some of the roots and over-wintering them in a greenhouse or cold frame.

E. WATERING AND FEEDING

Soft fruits must not be allowed to dry out, so water regularly. A drip system on a timer is ideal with twice-daily watering during the summer.

We feed our soft fruit plants with a liquid comfrey feed high in potassium during the summer and early autumn, mulch them each autumn with a mix of comfrey leaves, pine needles and grass cuttings from an unfertilised lawn and also add a winter sprinkling of wood ash.

If you still prefer to use manufactured chemical fertilisers, give plants a feed with a general fertiliser in the winter and in early spring give them a high-potassium feed.

If you can find a packet locally, an autumn dressing of slow acting bone meal is excellent.

F. COPING WITH COMMON PESTS AND DISEASES

When buying plants try and obtain virus-resistant cultivars.

Lay good straw under the leaves of strawberry plants in early spring to prevent fruits from being water-logged and therefore reduce the chance of rotting. It also keeps fruit above the soil so that they are not splashed by mud when it rains and they drain and dry quickly when the sun comes out. This reduces the chance of mould or slug and snail damage.

Spray plants monthly with neem to protect against insect infestations.

If birds start to peck out fruit and leaf buds in late winter or if they steal too many fruits, cover plants with netting or build a fruit cage to cover all soft fruit plants. See also section 5.2.

Raspberries can become mouldy after rain. Remove any mouldy fruit that occurs.

G. RECOMMENDED PRUNINGS

Blackcurrants fruit on the previous year's growth while redcurrants fruit on old growth. Therefore prune out old fruiting branches of blackcurrants immediately after harvesting but ensure that you leave all strong new shoots which will bear next year's fruit. On the other hand only thin out the weaker and crossing branches of redcurrants.

Gooseberry bushes need pruning to shape and to allow light into the centre of the plant. Prune when the buds start to swell in January or February.

How you prune raspberries will depend on the variety you planted. Autumn fruiting varieties fruit on new year's growth and therefore all old canes can be cut down to the ground. However, summer fruiting varieties fruit on the previous year's growth and therefore only definitely dead canes should be cut during the winter. If in doubt, prune as if summer fruiting.

Each autumn runners should be cut off maturing strawberry plants to expand the strawberry bed or replace tired old plants. It's worth changing them every three years.

See also section 4.12.

H. HARVESTING AND STORAGE

To enjoy soft fruits at their best, harvest and eat the same day. Excess harvests can be frozen or processed into jams for the winter. Strawberries and raspberries can also be dried in a food drier.

Early strawberries even for Christmas can be forced by covering some plants with cloches but cover the cloches overnight with fleece and woven wind break material during frosty nights.

4.8 VINE FRUITS

A. MAIN USES AND BENEFITS

The three vine fruits regularly grown in Spanish gardens are grapes, passion fruits and kiwis. All three can be usefully grown to cover walls, a porch or a gazebo as well as being trained along wires between posts. If you have room, grapes can also be grown as bushes.

From a food point of view the main benefits of each are:

Grapes. Fresh grapes and freshly pressed grape juice, diluted and with added herbs, provide immediate energy. Grape juice is a refreshing non-alcoholic drink, cold or hot. You can chew the pips (a good source of antioxidants) and it's fun to make home-made wine or raisins from your own grapes as many rural Spanish families still do.

Passion fruits. The ripe, fleshy fruit is refreshing cut open and eaten with a small spoon (yes, the pips are a nuisance) and the fresh or dried flowers make a refreshing infusion said to be good for mood swings.

Kiwi. A fruit full of vitamin C that can be eaten at any time as a snack, for breakfast or in a fruit salad.

B. TYPES OF FRUITING VINE AND CHARACTERISTICS

English, Spanish and botanical names	Form	TBT	THT	TPT
GRAPEVINE Vid *Vitis vinifera*	Vine or bush	April/May	July to Oct	W and S
PASSION FRUIT Pasionaria *Passiflora edulis*	Vine	April to Oct	June to Oct	W
KIWI Kiwi *Actinidia chinnesis*	Vine	April/May	Aug to Oct	W
KIWINI Kiwini *Actinidia arguta* **	Vine	MayJune	Aug/Oct	W

Notes
TBT = Typical blossom times; **THT** = Typical harvest times;
TPT = Typical pruning time; **PR** = Typical pest resistance;
DR = Typical drought resistance; **FR** = Typical frost resistance.

Typical planting heights above sea level (metres)					PR	DR	FR
< 200	< 400	< 800	< 1200	> 1200			
*	*	*	*	*	M	H	H
*	*				H	M/H	M
*	*				H	L	M
	*	*	*	*	H	L	H

H = High; **M** = Medium; **L** = Low.
W = Winter; **Spr** = Spring; **S** = Summer; **A** = Autumn.
** The kiwini is a hybrid with small, reddish fruit that form in bunches like plums. The fruit is thin-skinned, pipless and can be eaten whole.

Grape

Kiwi

C. CHOICE OF VARIETIES

Grapes - Typical uses of some of the more popular vines grown in Spain are listed in the chart.

VARIETY OF GRAPE	Main uses			
	Eating (1)	Juice (mosto)	Wine	Raisins
Aledo		*		
Cardinal	*			
Sultanina	*	*		
Moscatel	*	*	White	*
Sylvaner		*	White	
Macabeo		*	White	
Merseguera		*	White	
Cab. Sauvignon		*	Red	
Merlot		*	Red	
Monastrell		*	Red	
Tempranillo		*	Red	

Many people will also find some of the other varieties pleasant to eat fresh or as raisins.

Passion - All passion flower climbers tend to produce at least a few fruit in the Spanish climate, but the best for large size and number of fruit is the Passiflora edulis, in English normally called a passion fruit rather than passion flower plant.

Kiwi - Plants are normally just labelled kiwi but as already mentioned there is a hybrid kiwini which is more drought and frost-resistant than a normal kiwi. It has a smaller fruit but in bunches like plums.

D. WHERE TO PLANT

All can be grown in most regions of Spain but do best in full sun. The kiwi grows best in damper, slightly cooler areas similar to Galicia and in colder regions passion flowers need to be grown in large pots and taken inside during the winter. The good thing about grapevines is that they are very undemanding about the type of soil they are grown in, so if you have poor soils, whether in a valley or on a hillside, a small vineyard may be just the thing for you.

All can be trained to cover walls (preferably south-facing), porches and gazebos within the flower garden, or trained along wires around the vegetable plot or in a dedicated fruit growing area of the garden.

E. HOW TO PLANT TO GET OFF TO A GOOD START

Purchase strong healthy plants and prepare the ground well. Rather than digging a planting hole the size of the container in which the vine was purchased, dig a hole at least 50cm in diameter and 50cm deep. Then refill, mixing plenty of well-rotted compost and manure into the soil. Water well, allow to settle for a few days and then plant the vine in the centre. If you are planting more than one vine, plant them two metres apart. Unless growing grapevines as bushes, tie all vines to their training wires as soon as planted.

Kiwis and kiwinis are not bisexual so it is necessary to plant one male vine *(macho)* to each two female fruiting vines *(hembras)*. It's most practical to plant the male between the two female vines with a two to three-metre spacing.

F. WATERING AND FEEDING

Grapevines were traditionally reared on the poorest and driest soils where nothing else would grow. The growers hoped for some timely rain after planting new vines, just before flowering, to stimulate the formation of flowers and fruit. Until the early 1990s it was forbidden to irrigate commercial grapes in Spain, but authorised yields almost three times greater are now possible with the copious use of water and chemical fertilisers. But the result is often watery and lacking the wonderful taste of naturally grown, traditional grapes. After eating them a few times we planted more of our own vines to grow naturally.

If producing your own wine or raisins, it is preferable not to water when the fruits are swelling and ripening in order to build up the sugar level and taste as much as possible as the basis for making full-bodied wines. Grapevines actually require little feeding except for a light spring dressing of well-rotted compost or manure.

Passion fruits are very drought-resistant once established but it is best to keep the roots damp to stimulate the formation of large fruits. They need no feeding if planted in fairly good soil.

Kiwi roots need to be kept damp and an annual mulch of well- rotted compost or manure is beneficial.

G. COMMON PESTS AND DISEASES

Grapevines suffer fungal diseases under humid conditions. As a precaution it is wise to dust vines lightly with sulphur powder once a month from the time of their winter pruning in January or February until the time of harvest. Do this more frequently if problems occur, especially when the fruit is swelling and changing colour from green to red or black. It is best done in the early evening when there is no wind. The easiest way is to fill an old sock or stocking with the sulphur power and shake lightly over the vines. If your vines are trained over a gazebo or porch, tie the sock to the end of a stick and dust from a stepladder.

If it rains heavily when the grapes are ripening, sulphur alone may be ineffective so spray the vines with a dilute solution of copper sulphate to combat the fungi that can develop. To protect your eyes, wear goggles when using either sulphur or copper sulphate. If these products used by the growers of organic grapes don't work for you, ask for a specialist proprietary spray at your local agricultural cooperative.

Passion fruit normally give no problems.

Kiwis normally cause few headaches once they start to fruit.

H. RECOMMENDED PRUNINGS

Grapevines need careful pruning both when first planted and each winter and summer.

When first planted
All new vines need pruning but you first need to decide whether you are to grow them as bushes, standards, or cordons. If you plan to grow them over a porch or pergola to provide summer shade, the vines will need training as standards. For growing against sunny walls they are best trained as cordons and in vineyards you can train them as cordons or standards attached to wires or as stand-alone bushes. In all cases with the first pruning cut back to just above the fourth bud and then allow the plant to grow freely for a year.

End of first-year pruning
Prune first-year plants in February or March after the risk of frost as follows.

Bush. Cut back each of the four branches that have grown to leave four new buds.

Standard. Cut back as above if you purchase a standard plant, but if training one from scratch leave only one of the strong branches to grow and don't prune until it reaches the height of the porch or gazebo that will eventually support the maturing plant.

Cordons. Train the strongest branch along a wire fixed between posts or along a wall then cut back the growth on the wire to four buds, the fourth being below the branch to make it easier to tie up later growth. Cut off all other branches and preferably seal the cuts with pruning paint or a lump of clay.

Espalier or double cordons. Train the two strongest branches in the opposite directions along the supporting wires and then prune each as per cordons.

Second, third and subsequent winters

Continue to do the winter pruning in February or March.

Bush. Cut back the four eyes/buds on each of the four main branches, which by now will be thickening up, and seal the cuts.

Standards. Cut off above the first four eyes/buds above the height of the porch or gazebo and seal. Remove any lower growth to leave a bare trunk.

Cordons and espaliers. Cut back the main branches trained on wire to eight eyes/buds and seal the cuts. With careful pruning it is possible to train cordons and espaliers into two and three-level vines.

Summer pruning of all types

Cut out all shoots below the fruiting branches, non-flowering shoots and any weak leaders. When flowers are formed, pinch out the tips of the fruiting lateral branches. The main branches on all types can be allowed to grow to four or five metres. Prune these only to keep tidy and not too hard as the leaves are critical to the generation of nutrients by photosynthesis.

Passion fruit. Prune to keep shape during the growing season and, when dormant during the winter, shorten the vines and cut out any dead wood.

Kiwis. When mature, prune to stop vine becoming too straggly and thin out growth to stimulate more side branches.

I. HARVESTING AND STORAGE

Grapes will be ready for harvesting between July and the end of September, depending on the variety, the region they are grown in, exposure to sun and the altitude at which they are grown. The longer grapes are left on the vines the sweeter they will become. Bunches for eating can be covered with muslin bags during their last month of filling out and ripening to prevent attacks by insects, especially wasps. Bunches hung up on a wire in a cool garage or cellar can keep for some months. We understand that the university of Elche is seriously investigating the coating of grapes and other fruits with aloe vera to prolong their storage life.

To make **raisins,** lay the grapes out to dry in the sun on a terrace or in a conservatory or use a proprietary, electrically heated fan tray drier. In humid areas grapes drying in the fresh air will need covering or taking in at night.

When making **wine**, the longer you leave grapes on the vines before harvesting the higher the sugar content will become and therefore the higher the level of alcohol achievable during fermentation. You can tread your grapes or, if you have a large harvest, take them to the local wine press and either bring the juice home to ferment or arrange for the local bodega to process it for you.

Passion fruit should be picked as soon as they are ripe and eaten fresh. Flowers can be dried and used for infusions.

Kiwis straight from the plant are fantastic, but they are normally picked a few days before they are ripe and ripened in a bowl. Picked unripe, especially at the end of the season, they will store in trays in a cool cellar or in the fridge for weeks.

Local wine press

J. REPRODUCTION

All four vines can be propagated from cuttings. Grapevine cuttings are normally planted in the open ground or in deep pots while passion fruits and kiwis are best planted in pots. Passion fruits can also be grown from seed. See section 4.14.

Propagating grape vines

4.9 MELONS, PEANUTS AND RHUBARB

A. MAIN USES AND BENEFITS

This book would not be complete without including melons, peanuts and rhubarb, although they are often grown on vegetable plots because of their similar needs for soil with a high nutrient and humus content and watering.

Ripe melons are the basis of some wonderful starters and desserts and the skins can be candied. A slice is also a good way of quenching one's thirst when gardening in the summer, as are juiced water melons.

Peanuts can be eaten salted or unsalted as snacks, made into peanut butter and incorporated into a number of recipes.

Rhubarb can be used for desserts, made into jam and be frozen or bottled for winter use.

They can be grown within a cottage garden in large containers, within a vegetable plot or in a strip bed between rows of trees in an orchard.

B. TYPES OF MELONS AND CHARACTERISTICS

The following types of melon can be grown in gardens in Spain.

Water melon - the largest of the melon family can grow up to 50 centimetres in diameter although generally smaller. Red, pink and white-fleshed varieties are available. The colours of their skins range from dark green to light yellow striped to a motley, blotchy mix of colours. Can store for several months. We particularly like growing the smaller, sugar baby variety as excellent for just two people.

Cantaloupe melon - average-sized, yellow or orange flesh, perfumed and sweet. Do not store long.

Angel's hair melon - can grow to the size of a water melon. The creamy flesh forms as long strings resembling spaghetti within the shell and is used to prepare a number of sweet desserts and pastries. Can keep for months.

Ogen melon - small to medium-sized, round shape, green to yellow and even orange-coloured, very sweet and tasty. Does not keep. We love the Blenheim orange variety.

Piel de sapo/Pinonet melons -

both are hard-skinned green or greeny-yellow-striped ovals, very juicy and tasty. Stores well through to Christmas and beyond.

Amarillo Oro melons - soft, yellow-skinned, oval, only average in taste according to our taste buds and tend not to store well.

Our descriptions regarding taste and juiciness relate to fully ripe fruits picked no more than a day or two before eating. You will soon discover the delights of being able to harvest your own rather than eating the tasteless melons often sold in supermarkets and many restaurants.

Melons are fully ripe when the vine they are attached to withers and separates easily from the fruit. You will not need to resort to pressing into the ends, slapping it etc. to test if ripe as in markets (often one can't even do that in supermarkets).

All grow on plants that spread like vines across the soil. The smaller types can also be trained up cane frames provided the developing fruits are supported in nets.

Melons are not frost-hardy so direct sowing in the open is not possible until the last frosts are past. However, seeds can be sown a month before in a warm greenhouse.

C. HOW TO GROW MELONS

The success factors are as follows.

1. Obtain good seeds

This can be by retaining and drying seeds from a melon you particularly enjoyed for sowing the next spring or by buying packets of seeds. When buying seeds, check which the sellers use themselves and trust their choices for a year. If you are not satisfied, try a different variety and/or seed merchant the next year.

2. Prepare the soil ready for planting out

Melons are hungry, thirsty plants but do not like being actually wetted. It is therefore usual to either dig holes 50cm deep and 50cm across and fill these with a well-rotted compost/manure/earth mix around the end of the year. This will mean that, provided the filled holes and surrounding areas are well soaked with water in the spring before planting seeds or plantlets, the roots will have plenty of readily available natural nutrients and moisture. Make the holes three to five metres apart.

3. Grow strong seedlings

There are two ways of doing this:

• Sow two seeds in pots in a greenhouse six to eight weeks before last frosts normally occur so that strongly growing plantlets will be ready to plant out when the weather warms up.

• Sow five seeds in a mound of fine earth raised over the prepared holes two to four weeks before last frosts can be expected. Cover with a square wooden frame covered with a square of thick, clear plastic sheeting or plastic sheeting draped over two plastic or twig hoops and held down by earth heaped on the excess. When the plantlets are growing strongly and the weather has warmed up, remove the covers and trim off all but the two strongest-growing plants.

Note that you can sow seeds or plant out seedlings on the coastal strip up to four weeks earlier than in a sunny situation 350 metres above sea level in an inland valley 15 kilometres from the sea.

4. Just sufficient moisture

Before sowing seeds in the open or planting plantlets, thoroughly soak the prepared holes and surrounding areas by flooding or hose. Water seeds or plantlets well immediately after sowing/planting.

In very water-retentive soils it will not be necessary to water after the initial watering, provided the surface of the soil is regularly hoed to reduce capillary water evaporation to a minimum. Be careful not to damage shallow roots when hoeing. In other cases water the plants weekly to keep the deep, enriched soil damp without wetting the leaves or use a drip feed that operates every 48 hours.

Watering *Sandía*

Melons 'secano'

Melon Canteloupe

5. Supplementary feeds

If the vines are growing strongly and fruits fattening steadily, do nothing. If things are slow, give plants a rich potassium feed. We use a comfrey feed (see section 5.3).

6. Pruning the vines

To achieve larger melons when two or three healthy melons have formed on any branch of the spreading vine, remove other just-forming fruit and flowers.

110

7. Successive sowings
By planting seedlings from after the last frosts until August, one can harvest melons through to October or even November if the autumn is warm. Naturally early and late melons can be raised in cold frames or greenhouses as in northern Europe.

8. Disease prevention
Lightly dust the vines weekly with sulphur powder shaken through an old sock or stocking to prevent fungal attacks. Remove any affected dry leaves as they form and any diseased fruits.

9. Patience at harvest time
The best indication that a melon is at its best and ready to harvest is when the vine to which it is attached dies off and the connection to the melon separates naturally or with a light tap. You will discover this for yourself by trial and error.

　　If you have very heavy crops and are obviously going to have to store a good few, pick them about a week early and allow to ripen slowly in store. Unfortunately, this ripening by gentle decay is unlikely to result in as good a melon as those freshly harvested when fully sun-ripened.

10. Storing
Store in a cool dark place and check fruit every week or so. Melons can keep until Christmas and beyond.

D. HOW TO GROW PEANUTS

Peanuts like melons are not frost-hardy and require hot weather to germinate. We plant ours in late May and harvest in the early autumn - normally in mid-September. They can be grown successfully in the cottage garden, anywhere in containers, on any vegetable plot or as a strip bed between rows of fruit trees in the orchard.

The success factors are:

1. Use good seeds. The best are your own pods kept from year to year or obtained from a Spanish neighbour who has been growing them for years, second best are pods from a sack at a local agricultural cooperative or pet food shop. As a last resort buy a packet of unsalted peanut pods from a food store, but many may not germinate.

2. Prepare the soil by digging in plenty of well-rotted compost and soak the soil.

3. Make planting holes about 5-8cm deep and 30cm apart. Plant five peanuts separated from their pods in each hole. Fill holes with soil to bury peanuts, firm the surface and water. The peanuts should germinate and appear in about 10 to 14 days.

4. Then keep just-damp and well-weeded until the tops start to die back in the early autumn. Let the leaves brown and then dig up the harvest. Be careful to leave no pods in the soil. If the plants are over-watered, they will produce a lot of foliage instead of

111

pods and forming pods may rot.

5. Shake and brush off any soil, wash and dry the pods in the sun. Give a final drying in a low oven or fan dryer and then store in an airtight container. Before doing so, separate out some of the largest pods and store separately labelled "Peanuts for planting next spring".

6. If you want to salt peanuts before eating, separate from the pods and fry lightly in a little olive oil. When ready, tip on to a paper kitchen towel on a plate and shake on salt to taste.

HOW TO GROW RHUBARB

Unless you live in the cooler, wetter north, rhubarb *(ruibarbo)* is not easy to grow in Spain. In the warmer coastal strip and inland valleys one can be plagued by attacks of slugs which find the juicy stems to their liking during dry spells in the spring and the summer. If you cover the crowns with Victorian-style terra cotta forcing chimneys, the humid and cool conditions inside the chimneys also attract snails.

If you find some crowns or import them, the four main requirements are:

a. Enriched soil with annual manure mulch.

b. Plant in a shady situation as rhubarb bakes under the Spanish sun.

c. Continuous damp conditions.

d. Restricted light during main growing season, April to May. You can surround the crowns with a 40 to 50cm-high box, wide plastic/concrete tube or, if you are lucky, an imported old terra cotta Victorian rhubarb cloche filled with straw.

e. Continual attack on slugs and snails using Neem powder (www.trabe.com) or a circle of beer traps.

f. Harvest the young succulent stems regularly.

g. Cover with straw during winter.

4.10 SOIL PREPARATION

As mentioned previously, it pays off to spend time preparing the soil before you actually plant fruit trees, bushes and plants.

Rotovate or double-dig the soil. Add one or two plastic baskets of fully composted compost, plus half or a full basket of well-composted animal manure per square metre - either the one square metre required for each tree planted (see section 4.2F) or the entire orchard area. Doing this will:

a. Provide all the essential nutrients required for the natural growth of what you plant.

b. Improve the water-holding capacity of the soil and, most importantly, improve its drainage.

c. Reduce your water bills as less rain water or irrigation water will immediately drain through to the sub-soil, run off because the surface is hard-baked and impenetrable, or evaporate from the hard surface by capillary action.

d. Reduce the need to use large quantities of fertiliser each year (see section 5.3).

SOIL ACIDITY

One more thing is worth doing: check the acidity of your soil. Acidity is measured by its pH. This in turn is measured on a scale of 0 to 14, 7 being regarded as neutral. A measurement of 0 to 7 is regarded as acid and 7 to 14 as alkaline.

The scale is logarithmic so an acidity of 6.0 is 10 times as acid as one of 6.99 and likewise one of 5.0 is 10 times as acid as one of 6.0. On the alkaline side, 8.0 is 10 times as alkaline as 7.001.

Fruits grow best at a pH acidity level of 6.0 to 6.5, except for soft fruits which in general grow better in soils with a pH of 5.5 to 6.0.

If you are concerned that trees, bushes or plants are not performing well, even though you think you have fed and watered them satisfactorily, test your soil 10 and 20 centimetres below the surface with a pH metre, soil-testing kit or litmus paper. Acid levels can be raised by watering with collected rain water, adding slightly acid composts and manures and by sprinkling sulphur powder on the surface of the soil before rotovating. Beware: bags of worm compost, a popular organic fertiliser, can be alkaline.

Acidity levels can also be increased by irrigating with rainwater collected in a storage tank. Acidic composted pine needles can be added to the soil in which strawberries are to be planted.

If part of your soil has been contaminated accidentally by the backwash or emptying of your own or a neighbour's swimming pool, or as a result of your well having gone salty, you can wash out the contamination by spraying or flooding the area with good water.

However this may take time and the amount of water and number of treatments required will obviously be determined by the extent of the contamination and how quickly the water soaks down into the subsoil taking the contamination with it.

4.11 WATERING EFFECTIVELY

The watering needs of the various types of fruits have been indicated in section 4.2 to 4.9. In this section we discuss how the watering might be best achieved.

WHY WATERING IS REQUIRED

The moisture needs of the soil under and around fruit trees, bushes and plants are as follows:

113

1. Sufficient readily available water for the roots to absorb easily to:

• support the growth and rigidity of the cell structure of trunks, branches, leaves, flowers and fruit;

• keep the surface of leaves wet at night so that carbon dioxide can be extracted from the air to convert to chlorophyll;

• enable the processes associated with keeping the internal cell liquids cool or hot to be maintained at maximum efficiency;

• replace the moisture lost from the surface of the leaves through evaporation, which is increased by rising temperatures and falling barometric pressures.

2. Sufficient moisture to dissolve nutrients and minerals in the soil ready for the roots to extract. TerraCottem enriched compost can be worked into the soil.

3. Replacement of water lost from the soil surrounding the root balls as a result of: evaporation from the surface; drainage down to the lower strata of the soil, or out of the bottom of containers; and absorption of moisture by the surrounding drier, unwatered soils by a sponge effect. These factors reinforce the need to improve the structure of the soil before planting any fruit trees.

4. Water used by an undergrowth of weeds or in a cottage-style garden by low-growing plants under the trees.

Rain storms can meet all these needs for a while and less watering will be required during cooler winter and autumn months. However, unless you have improved the soil before planting and regularly hoe the surface, losses 3 and 4 above could well be very much greater than the water actually used by the trees, especially during the hotter months.

A. WATERING CONTAINERS OF ALL SORTS

If you have only one or two containers, a watering can will suffice although for convenience a mini irrigation system could be installed.

Once you have more containers, a handy hose or irrigation system is recommended. As illustrated, a number of companies including Hozelock now offer easily assembled kits. The photograph also shows a canister of TerraCotem gel which we recommend for mixing into the compost in the bottom half of containers to ensure that there is always a reservoir

of water should you forget to irrigate for a few days - or if the battery in the timer of your irrigation system fails and goes unnoticed for a few days. It's wise to change batteries every three months.

When filling and planting a strawberry barrel, push 3cm or 4cm plastic tubes into the compost, one almost to the bottom, one two-thirds of the way down and the last a third of the way down. If you water through these and on the surface by hose or irrigation system, you will be able to get water to the roots of all plants. A similar tube can be fitted in all containers.

Container-grown trees benefit from a mist spray of the leaves in the early evening during hot summer weather.

B. WATERING ROWS OR BLOCKS OF SOFT FRUITS

The shallow roots of soft fruits need to be moist at all times. If you use channelled water, flood down the rows weekly during spring, summer and autumn if there is no rain. Otherwise fix up an irrigation system using porous rubber or woven plastic tubing and, under dry conditions, water every other day. In each case the tubes wet a continuous strip of earth.

C. WATERING FRUIT TREES

If you only have a few trees in the garden, they can be watered with a watering can or hose. But you will need a number of watering cans or a good few minutes of hose-holding to ensure the water gets down to the lowest roots of even young trees in dry weather. It is therefore preferable to set up an irrigation system with a timer. As the trees grow, the point of watering will need to be gradually moved outwards so that you are always watering the soil just outside the drip line of each tree. This encourages the roots to grow longer. Deep watering down to below the lowest roots is also necessary to encourage the roots to go downwards searching for water. This is why a deep watering once a week is better than a shallow daily watering.

This is best achieved by using a drip irrigation system using 2cm or 3cm-bore plastic tubing with drips added where required or tubing with factory-fitted drip points at set intervals. We suggest you use tubing with sprays a metre apart, blocking off those not required.

The laying out of either type of piping for young, growing and mature trees is illustrated in the sketch. Drip irrigation systems are essential for absentee gardeners to ensure that young trees are not lost during their absence.

It is worth digging a hole near a drip point every so often to check how deep your watering penetrates. You can check the moisture level at various depths and at the same time the pH level with inexpensive hand-held metres.

For very mature trees you can purchase special drip irrigation systems the tubes of which can be buried a metre or more below the surface to ensure that all the water is delivered to where the roots can find it.

It is also possible to sink a number of 4cm-diameter plastic tubes long enough to reach the lower roots around any tree and water into these. Tubes 40cm long will be sufficient for young trees and up to 60 or 70cm for more mature trees.

Some growers will have to flood around their fruit trees from a channelled irrigation system. To minimise the amount of water used, it is wise to build a retaining bank around individual or rows of fruit trees just outside the drip line so the water penetrates the soil where required.

D. HOW MUCH AND HOW OFTEN

How much water fruit trees need is a vexed question

Many gardens are relatively small and dwarf or moderately sized trees are more easily accommodated than large specimens. Naturally, the more you water trees the quicker they will grow and the larger the tree will eventually be, but if they become waterlogged they can soon suffer fungal diseases. On the other hand in most areas many mature trees of many types will survive even if very rarely watered or indeed not at all. But they may not produce reliable fruit crops.

They may also become stressed and susceptible to diseases if they are not correctly watered and fed.

Flooding papaya plant

EXTENT OF WATERING	HIGH	HIGH (1)	MEDIUM	HIGH (1)
	MED	MEDIUM	LOW	MEDIUM
	LOW	HIGH (3)	MEDIUM	HIGH (2)
		LOW	MEDIUM	HIGH
			EXTENT OF FEEDING	

The table illustrates the extent of risks to young trees, as follows.

High (1): High or excessive watering with no pre-preparation of soil before planting and little follow-up feeding (see section 5.3) is likely to lead to forced weak growth, which is vulnerable to disease and pests as well as requiring an unnecessary amount of pruning (see section 4.12). Roots can also rot if waterlogged.

High (2): High or excessive feeding with chemical fertilisers with little or no watering will inevitably result in roots being burnt and stunted growth.

High (3): Trees planted in soil that has not been improved and are never or rarely watered are likely to become stressed and stunted. You will find yourself cutting out diseased and even dead branches within a couple of years.

Low: Moderate watering and feeding by preparing the soil as explained in previous sections creates the best balanced environment for young trees and those trees that need to be watered when they are mature such as citrus. The use of supplementary feeds is discussed in section 5.3. Other trees such as almonds, figs and olives can have their watering and feeding cut back to zero as they mature.

What volumes of water you actually use will depend on:

• How well you improved the soil before planting trees.

• The slope of your land and whether you have channelled it to avoid run-off during watering and rainfalls.

• The seasonal pattern of rainfall in your area and the temperatures experienced.

• Whether you have kept the surface of the soil loose to reduce to a minimum capillary evaporation, especially in clayey soils.

• Whether you are watering for the first time that year or doing a regular watering.

• Whether you have planted appropriate or inappropriate trees for your area. For instance, if you plant a pear tree unnaturally in a garden next to the sea in Marbella in Andalusia, it will need much more watering than if planted in its natural habitat around Lleida in Aragon.

At the top end of water usage a commercial grower of citrus fruits in the Valencia or Murcia regions using a drip irrigation system might irrigate each maturing tree in an orange grove daily with 20 litres of water during the spring, 40 litres of water during the summer, and 20 during the autumn. Obviously, amounts would be reduced or watering halted for a few days after heavy storms.

A similar grower watering by flooding a mature grove from a channelled water supply will typically flood every 28 days from the time flower buds start to form until harvest time, increasing this to every 21 days in a particularly hot dry summer. The first watering of the year might be equivalent to 60 litres of water per tree as the soil is very dry and from then onwards each watering would be equivalent to 25 to 40 litres a tree per day, depending on the temperatures between each watering.

Younger trees might well require:

2 litres a day if one to two years old

4 litres a day if four years old.

10 litres a day if eight years old

In a typical garden it is usual to use less than these amounts for citrus trees and deciduous fruit trees, for one is normally aiming for moderate-sized trees with a long-fruiting life span and reasonable crops, rather than fast-maturing trees that yield enormous crops until they are 25 years old, which are then uprooted and replaced. In our holistic garden (see section 1.7) fruit trees are treated like any other shrub or tree. What we ensure is that they are watered, if it has not rained for a while, when flower buds start to swell, open and set fruit and especially when the fruits first start to swell to prevent an excessive fruit fall. By the way, some fruit fall is normal. It's nature's way of getting rid of weak fruits and an excess to ensure reasonable-sized fruits. As explained earlier, other forming fruit can be removed by hand to further increase the size of the remaining fruit without extra watering. This makes more nutrients available for each forming fruit and is a better way to increase the size of home-grown fruits than by extra watering. Often large fruits produced by pumping in extra water lack the flavour of fruits grown under more natural conditions.

Our deep-rooted mature fig, quince, olives, almonds, pomegranate, apricot and grapes are never watered but young mangoes, avocado and maturing citrus trees are on a general garden irrigation system with their jets more open than for other plants.

What we water is governed by what the trees look like and the size of our summer water bill. And the best way of controlling that is to grow fruits compatible with the climate of the area in which you live.

Some dry areas of Spain now have significant shortages of water because developers are building houses and golf courses etc. where no one lived before and new residents are planting thirsty types of fruit trees, which were either never grown there owing to the lack of water or the orchards were abandoned when wells went dry or salty.

SOME GENERAL FACTORS AFFECTING THE NEED FOR WATER

Factors that increase need for water	Factors that decrease need for water
No prior improvement of soil	Well-prepared soil
Very large trees planted	Dwarf cultivars planted
Drought conditions	Have just had a storm
Scorching dry winds	Calm cool days
Temperatures above 35 degrees	Temperatures rarely above 25 degrees
Hard-baked soil	Deep soil
Cracked soil	Rich high in humus soil
Shallow, stony soil	High water table - easy for roots to find water
Sandy soil	
Low water table	Trees planted through black plastic sheeting and mulched with stone chippings
Under-planting with thirsty plants	
Too much nitrogen-rich fertiliser	Ground underneath always loosened
Trees exposed to strong winds	Soil enhancers such as TerraCottem mixed into soil
Closely planted trees	

E. WHEN TO WATER DURING DAY

We suggest you water in the morning during the autumn and winter to ensure that any surface water has drained away in case of night frosts and during the evening during the spring and summer so that most

119

water soaks into the soil, there are minimum evaporation losses and less chance of the surface of the soil baking to an impermeable cake, which it can do after daytime rain or watering.

F. A FILTER IS USEFUL

The photograph below shows a coarse and fine filter fitted to our water inlet pipe. We fitted this a few years ago to ensure that small grit did not enter the irrigation tubes and block up the jets on a regular basis.

G. ADDING FERTILISERS

If you have a pumped or gravity irrigation system, it is possible to add accurately measured quantities of fertiliser to irrigation water on a daily or continuing basis.

H. IMPROVING POOR-QUALITY WATER

Small direct osmosis desalination plants are available, sometimes from swimming pool supply shops, to enable water from saline wells to be used for watering fruit trees.

Vi-aqua (www.viaqua.ie) is a technology developed to improve the "wetability" of water and therefore reduce the amount used for irrigation.

GrosseGIE (www.agua-viva.info) is a technology for improving the healthiness of any water for human consumption and garden use.

I. SAVING RAIN WATER

Unfortunately, many modern houses are built without roof guttering and a large storage tank under the house or in the garden. This is a shame as natural rainwater is preferable to chlorinated town water for irrigating the garden. So we suggest that guttering be fitted to at least one roof slope and that one or more tubs or tanks are set up as storage tanks. This not only ensures a source of water if there are bans on the use of town water for garden irrigation, but rain is usefully slightly acidic and will also reduce your water bills.

J. LAST RESORTS

If water bans continue, consider using ecological washing agents and divert waste water from the washing machine and dishwasher to a holding tank to cool and settle before using for irrigation. Likewise, shower and bath water could be run to the same or a separate holding tank. Check local council regulations before you do so.

Efficient bio-digesters are now available that allow household waste waters to be puri-fied and recycled to the garden or orchard. In rural areas you could also install an eco loo to provide enough irrigation water for a few fruit trees in containers.

A swimming pool can provide the largest source of water. So stop adding chlorine, acid or salt and, when the readings are down to zero for chlorine and salt and the pH is below 7, use the water for irrigation. A few goldfish will soon deal with any mosquito larvae that appear and some oxygenating pond weed will help keep the water clean and provide a good habitat for the fish.

4.12 PRUNING YOUR FRUIT TREES, BUSHES AND PLANTS

A. INTRODUCTION

Pruning fruit trees is a necessary job but one of the most time-consuming, especially if you have a large number of mature trees grafted on vigorous root stocks. Some need to be pruned during the summer, others in January and February as part of the general garden cutback, while others are best left until after the chance of spring frosts are past. The general guidelines listed here and the chart are based on our experience. Much has been learned by watching and chatting to elderly Spaniards while they pruned their orchards and groves.

If you are not experienced in the art and have many trees - especially if you have an orange, olive or almond grove - consider taking on help. Or arrange for somebody to prune the trees for you on the understanding that they have the right to a major portion of the fruit at harvest time.

B. SOME GENERAL GUIDELINES

1. Decide on the shape of tree you wish to have in your garden before doing any pruning. The possibilities were illustrated in section 4.1. In theory any tree can be pruned to any shape, but some will be more successful than others. The most popular shapes of trees are listed in the table that follows later in this section.

2. The pruning of young, newly planted trees should be minimised in the first couple of years to allow the trees to concentrate on developing strong far-reaching root structures rather than new energy-sapping growth.

3. Debate continues between commercial growers who prune heavily and ecological fruit growers who minimise pruning. The first aim at the largest crop of the largest fruit possible, even if it tires the tree out to the point where it must be changed (every 25 years for oranges). The ecological growers aim to prolong the productiveness of their trees for as many years as possible. Orange trees can produce for centuries and 2,000-year-old olive trees exist in Spain. In the table we take a balanced approach, somewhere between the two.

4. There are four types of pruning, each carried out at a different time of the year. Winter pruning when the trees are dormant. This is the time to remove large-diame-

Pre-pruned plum

Pruned plum

Plum blossom

ter excess and diseased branches and to coppice old chestnut trees and the centre branches of trees with dense evergreen foliages, such as citrus and olive, to allow air and sun into the centre of the tree.

Early spring pruning when leaf and flower buds start to swell. At this stage fruiting spurs are trimmed back on some trees (e.g. almond and apple) and whole branches on others (e.g. orange and olive) in order to reduce the quantities of fruit and increase the size of those which will develop.

Early summer pruning when forming fruit can be thinned out to increase the size of the fruit left on the trees.

This can also be assisted by cutting out unnecessary vigorous non-fruiting growth so that the sap/nutrients are used to swell fruit rather than increase the foliage.

Summer pruning of some deciduous trees after fruit has been harvested to stimulate the development of flower/fruit buds for the following year.

The balance between the four types of pruning varies for different types of fruit trees. This is reflected in the guidelines given in sections 4.2 to 4.9 and the table that follows in this section.

5. The overall benefits of the combined pruning and thinning are listed below.

a. To improve the shape of the tree as a feature, to give better shade, to open up a vista, or to train the tree to hide the house next door.

b. To achieve a good balance between old and new growth.

c. To create special formats such as cordons, fans, umbrellas and standards.

d. To reduce the height of fruiting branches to make harvesting possible without a ladder.

e. To reduce the stress on the root system if in bad soil.

f. To improve garden hygiene by cutting out dead, diseased or pest-covered branches and leaves.

g. To stimulate fruiting side shoots and fruit buds.

Pruning side shoots

Un-pruned grapevine

Pruned grapevine

h. To improve the size of fruit by diverting rising sap from the creation of new growth to swelling fruit and by reducing the number of fruit left on a tree to maturity.

i. To allow ventilation and reduce humidity in the centre of the tree to prevent diseases.

j. To remove crossing branches that reduce the amount of sun on fruit and make harvesting awkward.

k. To enable the sun to shine on ripening fruit by cutting out the centre and excessive leaf cover on the end of branches.

l. To allow space between trees or between a tree and path or terrace

m. To prevent long branches from breaking from an over-load of fruit or strong winds.

n. To give other plants light.

6. The table that follows in section C provides basic guidelines for the pruning of the various types of fruiting tree, bush or plant that you are likely to have in your garden.

7. The extent of pruning will be affected by a number of factors including the following.

Factors that can increase amount of pruning required during the year	Factors that can decrease amount of pruning required during the year
A vigorous root stock	A dwarfing root stock
Excess watering	Moderate to low watering
Excess feeding	Moderate to low feeding
Choice of large types of tree	Choice of small types of tree
Pruning rarely	Annual pruning

8. Well-prepared and planted trees will develop a natural form and growth rate appropriate to your microclimate.

9. Over-pruning can upset a tree's balance between growth supported by nutrients extracted from the soil and those from the air by photosynthesis.

10. Poor pruning and hacking at a tree can allow diseases to enter.

11. Large-diameter cuts need sealing with a proprietary pruning sealer or clay.

12. Cordons, espaliers and fans are trained along wires against walls or trellis as pruning alone could not create the forms.

13. The main pruning is done during the winter months when a tree or vine is dormant or just when the sap is starting to rise and buds starting to swell.

14. Summer pruning is restricted to thinning fruit, removing diseased growth, stimulating fruiting side shoots for the next year and maintaining ornamental shapes.

15. It is preferable to remove fruit from new trees for two or three years until it has grown a good root system and substantial network of branches. Early fruit is often there because a mature branch was grafted on to a young rootstock while root system development is still too immature to support fruit crops in addition to the priority of developing a strong, healthy framework of branches and leaves.

16. Always prune with good-quality, sharp tools. The tools we recommend are illustrated.

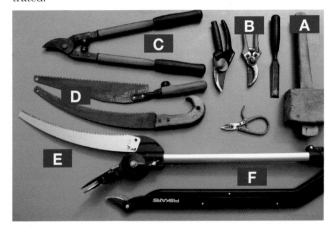

The various tools are used as follows.

A. A mallet and broad chisel for pruning citrus trees.

B. Small pruners for light pruning.

C. Heavy pruners for heavier work.

D. Saws for cutting through medium and large branches.

E. A combined extendible pruner and saw to cut out high branches.

F. A long, single-handed pruner which is very useful for getting to the centre of trees and cutting prickly blackberry and gooseberry bushes.

17. Always disinfect the blades of tools in diluted bleach or a mild disinfectant to reduce the chance of transferring diseases from one tree to another.

18. Clean and sharpen tools on a regular basis to ensure clean cuts.

19. Don't climb into trees to prune but use a stable design of step ladder. A runged ladder against branches can do damage.

20. Clean away all prunings from under trees and ensure that anything diseased is burned. Long, straight prunings are useful to support peas etc and shorter ones, once dried, as kindling in a wood-burning stove.

21. Wide umbrella fig, carob, cherry, olives and walnut trees can be trained by hanging weights to weigh young branches down. The weights are increased gradually as the branches thicken and all upward growing branches kept short to provide a central canopy.

Weighted olive tree.

C. GUIDELINES FOR PRUNING A VARIETY OF FRUIT TREES, BUSHES AND PLANTS

TYPE OF FRUIT TREE	FRUIT TREES IN GROUP	FRUIT FORMS ON...	TYPICAL PRUNING SHAPES	ANNUAL PRUNING REQUIRED *Apply to all stone fruits except olives*
STONE	Plum	One or two-year branches	Flat umbrella, wine glass, fan or cordon	Light summer pruning to keep shape, to stimulate next year's fruit buds and to keep height down for picking
	Cherry & apricots	Side shoots and one-year wood	Open wine glass, fan or free-growing	Cut out suckers at base as they appear and low-down, weak branches. Cut out deadwood and crossing and dangerous branches in winter.
	Peach & nectarine	One-year fruiting shoots and main branches	Wine glass, fan shape or free	Late spring/early summer thin out forming fruits to produce larger fruits. Cut out main shoots on cherry trees when 1 to 1.5 metres long to encourage side branches.
	Níspero	One-year laterals and tips	Wineglass or standard	For apricots lightly trim and shorten old branches to stimulate new laterals. Cut out fruited shoots. Leave one-year growth and trim to shape.
	Avocado	On maturing wood	Free form bush or standard	Prune out fruited shoots of peach and nectarine after harvesting.
	Olives	On young branches	Standard with 1, 2, 3 or 4 trunks as per local tradition	Olives are treated differently. They are often cut back very hard to keep tree low to ease harvesting. They are also thinned by cutting out up to 50 per cent of branches in late winter. If allowed to grow freely, can reach very large size and live 2,000 years.

GUIDELINES FOR PRUNING A VARIETY OF FRUIT TREES, BUSHES AND PLANTS

TYPE OF FRUIT TREE	FRUIT TREES IN GROUP	FRUIT FORMS ON...	TYPICAL PRUNING SHAPES	ANNUAL PRUNING REQUIRED
PIPPED	Citrus	One year branches and new shoots	Standard, bush, wine glass or bastion as a hedge	Oranges, mandarins and grapefruits. In February/March cut off low suckers, remove dead wood and cut out upward-growing centre branches every two or three years to improve aeration. See section 4.2 for more detailed description of possibilities. Continuously fruiting varieties of lemon are best pruned at the end of a crop cycle as the next batch of flowers are appearing. Grapefruits will produce larger fruits if you trim back ends of fruiting branches to fruit buds and thin fruit when formed
	Pears	On ends of new shoots and side shoots	Cordon, espalier, fan or pyramid	Cut back woody branches to stimulate fruiting side shoots. Trim to fruit buds
	Apples	As above	As above	Cut out suckers and small crossing branches. Trim two-thirds of laterals back to fruit buds each year
	Quince/ Membrillo	One year growth and side shoots	Standard	Prune lightly back to fruit buds. Cut off roots' suckers as they appear

GUIDELINES FOR PRUNING A VARIETY OF FRUIT TREES, BUSHES AND PLANTS

TYPE OF FRUIT TREE	FRUIT TREES IN GROUP	FRUIT FORMS ON...	TYPICAL PRUNING SHAPES	ANNUAL PRUNING REQUIRED
SEEDY	Fig	At the leaf nodes on new and one-year growth	Free form standard, wine glass, fan on wall or flat umbrella	When young, cut out central shoot to encourage future horizontal growth. Cut out old wood to reduce height and stimulate fruiting forks and branches. Can be ruthless with an old tree to reshape (see photographs)
	Persimmon	Young branches less than one year old	Free form standard	Prune to reduce crop after fruit has set to stimulate larger fruits
	Kiwi	One-year growth	Cordon, espalier, or free form	Cut out fruited branches and in early spring reduce the amount of excess vegetation
	Grapes	On new growth	Cordon, espalier or umbrella	During summer cut out excess green growth below forming fruit, non-fruiting growth and weak leaders and thin-forming bunches. Cut vines back to four buds per framework branch in February/March after frosts. See section 4.8H for more detailed guidelines.
	Passion fruit	On new growth	Train over wall or gazebo	Prune to keep tidy. In small gardens cut back top growth in winter to prevent becoming straggly
NUTS/ BEANS	Almonds	On one-year growth and side shoots	Standard	Cut out unnecessary main branches in December to create a well-shaped tree with airy centre. Prune out one-year growth and older side shoots with no flower buds just as buds begin to swell. This will vary from December in the south to February or even March if high up in the north. Prune out excessive vertical new growth during summer to increase size of nuts.

GUIDELINES FOR PRUNING A VARIETY OF FRUIT TREES, BUSHES AND PLANTS

TYPE OF FRUIT TREE	FRUIT TREES IN GROUP	FRUIT FORMS ON...	TYPICAL PRUNING SHAPES	ANNUAL PRUNING REQUIRED
NUTS/ BEANS	Walnuts	Standard	Free form standard, wine glass, fan on wall or flat umbrella	Normally left to grow naturally. Trim to shape when young.
	Carob	On old wood One-year growth	Standard or columnar	Carob trees were traditionally pruned as fat columns with equal width and height of foliage. The effect can be very attractive.
	Hazel	On side shoots	Standard or bush	Trim to shape, especially if grown as a hedge. Cut off root suckers twice a year.
	Pistachio	On side shoots	Standard	Trim to shape and cut out crossing branches. Shorten branches after fruiting to stimulate fruiting side shoots.
SOFT	Strawberries	On new growth	Low plants	Cut out dead leaves and stems as they appear. Cut off runners in the autumn and transplant to replace three-year plants.
	Raspberries	On new canes	Cordons	Cut out dead fruiting canes during the winter. See Section 4.7H for detailed instructions. Trim any frost-burnt tips in the spring.
	Redcurrants/ whitecurrants	On old wood	Bush or cordon	Cut out crossing branches to let air and light into bush. Trim back lateral branches to second bud in winter to stimulate fruit buds on old wood.
	Blackcurrants	On previous year's growth	Bush or cordon	For first four years cut back main branches by a third each winter and cut out crossing branches. Later, cut out some old branches to stimulate growth after fruiting.

GUIDELINES FOR PRUNING A VARIETY OF FRUIT TREES, BUSHES AND PLANTS

TYPE OF FRUIT TREE	FRUIT TREES IN GROUP	FRUIT FORMS ON...	TYPICAL PRUNING SHAPES	ANNUAL PRUNING REQUIRED
SOFT	Gooseberries	One year and older side shoots	Bush or cordon	Prune like a miniature plum tree. Encourage upward growth. Cut off downward growing branches. A 25-per-cent pruning is normal
	Blackberries/ loganberries and tayberries	On new growth	Cordons, fan or espalier	Cut back hard fruited branches and remove weak suckers
	Blueberries	Side shoots	Low bush	Cut out any dead twigs
OTHER	Bananas	On flowering central stalk	Left to grow naturally	Cut out old leaves and fruited stalks. Leave to grow as a clump or split of plantlets. It's advantageous to mulch with the prunings

D. REGENERATIVE PRUNING OF OLD TREES

If you inherit old, neglected, non-productive trees, the best thing is to cut back all the main branches that show any sign of life to 20 to 50cm stumps at the end of winter after frosts. Then dig the soil around the tree to a fork depth and soak the soil. Then apply a light dressing of ecological fertiliser high in nitrogen and soak a second time.

The alternative is to cut the trunk down to a stump and graft on young cuttings. This is discussed in section 4.13.

4.13 THE ANCIENT ART OF GRAFTING

When the layout and planting of your garden is almost finished you may have the time and inclination to have a go at grafting. It can be an interesting but frustrating pastime until you have developed the knack.

But first: what is grafting? The improvement or production of a new tree or shrub by the joining of a leaf bud or cutting from a donor tree to another "host" tree so that the graft joins inseparably to the host and then starts to grow as a new limb. The cuttings to be grafted are termed "scions" and the host to which the scions will be grafted "rootstock".

A. WHY GRAFT?

There are several reasons you may want to learn to graft.

1. To add additional branches to an otherwise sparse tree.

2. To replace the existing main branches on an old tree which still has a healthy trunk.

3. The challenge and fun of creating multi-fruiting fruit trees or vines. You can, for example, add branches of:

- plum to an almond tree
- lemon and grapefruit to an orange tree
- pear and apple to a quince tree
- peach to a nectarine
- white grape to a black vine
- sweet orange to a sour Seville orange.

4. The propagation of new, vigorous, full-size trees or less vigorous dwarf trees by joining cuttings and rootstocks of different cultivars of one family of fruit.

5. The changing of the cultivars of a fruit tree, e.g. the grafting of a good fruiting variety of a pear or avocado on the strong trunk and root system of a more poorly fruiting variety.

6. Most fruit trees do not reproduce well from seed but often revert to one of the parent trees from the original breeding or even to a wild form. But the root stocks may provide an excellent root stock for grafting a cultivated variety.

7. Cuttings from many varieties of fruit trees do not root well.

8. The production of interesting and unusual forms of trees, e.g. a hedge or windbreak of inter-connected apple trees welded together where their branches cross to create a strong matrix structure.

9. The challenge, fun and satisfaction.

B. TYPES OF GRAFTS

There are five ways of joining scions and rootstocks:

1. Grafting buds to branches or trunks.

2. Grafting cuttings to main branches or trunks.

3. Grafting cuttings to side branches.

4. Grafting a cutting to a length of root.

5. Surface bonding between branches of the same tree or of different trees.

The professional fruit tree breeders and nurseries use a number of methods of varying complexity and ease for each type of graft. We describe here the grafts normally attempted by amateurs. They should be possible using the sketch and methods described.

C. BASIC GUIDELINES FOR MAKING THE GRAFTS

1. BUDDING. There are two basic types of bud graft. A bud can be grafted on to any healthy branch of a tree to create a better shape or to add a branch of another variety of fruit.

131

And a new tree can be formed by grafting one or more buds to a specially grown rootstock, which has been produced from a variety easily propagated from seed or cuttings. In both cases the graft is most easily made by a "T" graft, as follows.

    • Cut a 2cm "T" in the bark of the receiving rootstock and carefully ease the bark back to the cambium layer - the layer of cells between the bark and internal wood fibres which by cell division create both new bark tissue and new wood tissue as a tree grows.

    • Select and cut off a healthy side branch from the donor tree which has well-developed but still dormant leaf buds.

    • Select the strongest bud from the centre of the branch to prepare for grafting. Cut the branch half a centimetre on either side of the bud and then cut across the bark and ease off the outer bark with the bud in the centre. Then cut around the bud to create a triangular scion 1cm across and 2cm long.

    • Slide the scion into the ready-prepared "T" cut on the host tree. You are aiming for a perfect fit so you may need to enlarge the "T" slightly or trim the scion before completing the graft. If the join is perfect, no tying will be required. But the amateur grafter is recommended to tie the join together. The tie can then be waxed as a final precaution, but with cooling not hot wax. If the graft takes, the tie can be removed within a few weeks.

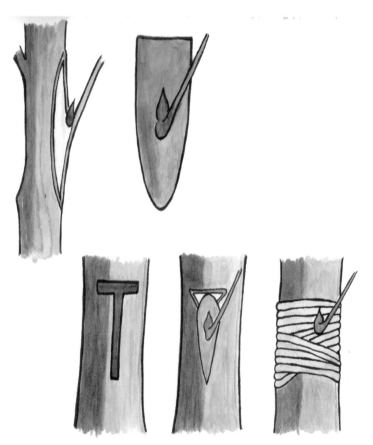

2. CUTTINGS

Cuttings can be grafted on to the trunk or the main branch of a tree that is to be improved in shape or to the top of a truncated rootstock cut off between 30cm and a metre above the ground.

a. Trunk or main branch grafts

• Cut off a healthy but as yet dormant side branch from the selected donor tree. Cut off the top where the diameter is about that of a pencil by making a centimetre-long sloping cut. Rub off any flower buds but leave leaf buds.

• Make a sloping vertical cut through the bark and cambium layer into the wood at the chosen grafting point on the host tree.

• Slip the scion firmly into the cut, wrap tape round to close the join and cover with wax.

b. Grafting cuttings to the top of a stump

• Cut the existing top crown of branches off a young tree to which you intend to graft a different cultivar or off an old healthy trunk where the crown of branches are past their best fruiting years and to which you want to graft the same or a different cultivar.

133

• Prepare the top of the rootstock trunk by either making three or four 2 to 3cm-long incisions around the circumference of the side of the top of the severed rootstock and easing the bark open; or by cutting a deep "V" across the top of the trunk or two such cuts to form an "X" on a larger trunk.

• Prepare and fit the scions as follows:

1. Cut three or four cuttings of equal diameter and length. Make a cut two-thirds across each cutting and then a 2 to 3cm sloping cut down the cutting so that it will fit exactly into the prepared incisions in the stock. Insert the cutting so that the notch sits on top of the rootstock when the end fits firmly into the cut. Tie around the top of the rootstock trunk.

2. Or cut the end of the cuttings as a wedge to fit tightly into the "V" cuts. A single scion can be cut and fixed into the "V" cut on a young rootstock.

The above methods can also be used to graft one or two cuttings on to a large diameter branch that has been cut back. To prevent diseases spoiling the grafts, seal the top of the trunk with a pruning sealing paint or, to be traditional, with a lump of wet clay.

3. GRAFTING CUTTINGS ONTO SIDE BRANCHES

- Choose a side branch on to which you want to graft a different variety or cultivar, e.g. a cutting of plum to an almond tree or a lemon to an orange tree.
- Take a cutting from a donor tree of the same thickness as the above side branch.
- Cut a 3cm sloping cut through the cutting and the branch to which it is to be joined where it is the same thickness as the cutting.
- Immediately place the two cut surfaces together, bind and cover with wax.

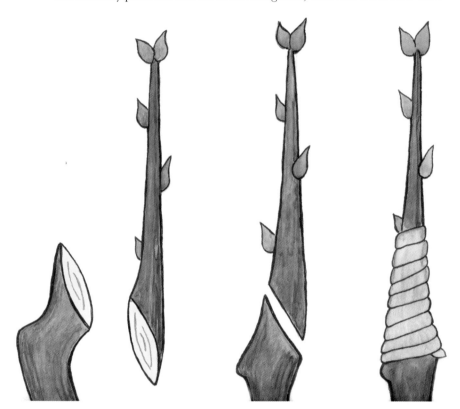

4. ROOT GRAFTS

Root grafts are made by digging up the root ball of a one or two-year-old seedling grown from seed - perhaps in a pot - and cutting off the strongest roots. A 3cm sloping cut is then made at the top of each length of root. A matching cut is then made on the base of a cutting taken from the tree that you want to graft on. The bare faces of the two cuts are held exactly together while they are bound with grafting tape. The bound join is best sealed in wax. The newly grafted tree should be immediately planted so that it does not dry out. Ensure that the graft is 2 to 4cm above the level of the earth and that the earth is raised up as a cone around the top of the root.

5. SURFACE BONDING

This is generally done to create a matrix tree or a solid screen by bonding two or more cordon trees of the same type of fruit, e.g. oranges, apples and pears. Cut off the bark between two crossing branches. Immediately tie the two surfaces together and cover the join with wax. With luck the two branches will soon unite.

THE SEVEN SUCCESS FACTORS

1. Timing. The grafting of cuttings is normally carried out in late February or March when the sap of the host tree or root stock is starting to rise. Budding is normally carried out when the host tree is still in a growth mode, but after harvesting the fruit. Joining of the branches of adjacent trees is best done in the spring.

2. Good tools and materials. Ensure that the knife you use is sharp and clean. Use special grafting wax or bees' wax (a candle can be melted down) and polyethylene tape that has some stretch and is flat. A roll of professional grafting tape is not expensive.

3. Hygiene. Ensure that sterile knives, clean wax and clean grafting ties are used.

4. Exclusion of any air bubbles between the scion and host by careful cutting and test-fitting before finalising the graft. If it does not seem to be 100 per cent correct, it's best to start again.

5. Removal of any ties as soon as a graft union has formed so as not to constrain the natural growth of the grafted cutting or scion.

6. Pruning of new growth the following spring to stimulate side shoots and flowering buds.

7. Only graft trees from the same or closely related families, e.g. lemons on orange trees but not plum trees, but plums graft well to almond trees.

HOW TO AVOID TYPICAL PROBLEMS

1. Air, disease or water gets into the join. Careful cutting and tight joining essential.

2. The buds dry out and don't develop. Ensure that you select fat buds from the middle of branches and use immediately.

3. Grafted cuttings die back. As soon as cuttings are cut, place the cut ends in non-chlorinated water to prevent the sap from starting to dry out before the cuttings are grafted.

4. Bud grafts are made too late so that sap retreats from the host branches before the graft is sealed.

5. Cutting grafts are made too early before the sap starts to rise. Do a new graft if a grafted cutting starts to die or go dry.

6. If you have no luck with bud grafts, try cutting grafts and vice versa.

7. Ensure that the roots of root ball grafts are kept moist and give a weak nitrogen feed fortnightly to stimulate leaf growth.

4.14 PROPAGATION OF FRUIT TREES, BUSHES AND PLANTS

Many fruit trees, bushes and plants can be propagated by the keen gardener to start off with or later to expand what is grown. Here are some examples:

A. FROM CUTTINGS

Many trees can be propagated by planting one or two-metre cuttings from healthy mature trees in the spring. For starters try doing this with a fig or walnut tree. Plant the ends of the cuttings 50cm deep. Keep damp. The cuttings can be planted in a nursery bed as illustrated or in their final situations in the garden.

Likewise, redcurrant and gooseberry bushes and grape vines are readily propagated from cuttings from well-hardened, one-year mature branches.

There are three ways of growing from such cuttings.

• Make a 30cm-deep slit trench with a spade. Take 50cm cuttings and slide 30cm into the trench. Water, back-fill with soil and form the surface. Leave for a year before transplanting into containers or open ground. Keep the soil just damp at all times.

• Do as above in deep containers.

• Place 30cm cuttings in dark-coloured wine or beer bottles filled with water. Plant in containers or open soil when good root systems have developed.

When you take cuttings, cut the base just below a leaf bud and cut off the top just above a leaf bud. Leave only a few buds at the top and rub off all others.

As explained in section 4.13, cuttings can also be grafted on rootstocks of similar types of fruit trees. See section 4.6 for how to propagate pineapples from the green top of a pineapple fruit.

B. FROM RUNNERS

Strawberries can be very easily propagated in the autumn by separating the young plantlets that form on long stems out of the heart of a maturing plant. The plantlets can be planted first in pots or planted directly into the ground in their final positions. In the latter case we suggest they are planted through holes in black plastic sheeting, as already referred to in section 4.11.

Within a couple of years suckers will start growing alongside a row of raspberries. Merely dig them up and plant to extend the existing row or start a new row.

Quince trees give out more suckers than most trees. These can be dug up and cut off from the main root from the tree and planted in a nursery bed or final position.

C. FROM SEEDS

Many fruit trees can be grown from seed, but due to genetic breeding many will not develop exactly as the variety from which the seed was kept. However, the roots of your self-grown tree can often provide a good rootstock on which a cutting from a good fruiting tree can be grafted (see section 4.13).

One never knows what will happen. One person might grow a fast-developing avocado tree which fruits wonderfully after five or six years and a neighbour might do the same and the tree never produces flower or fruit.

Propagating strawberries

Avocado from seed

Olive from seed

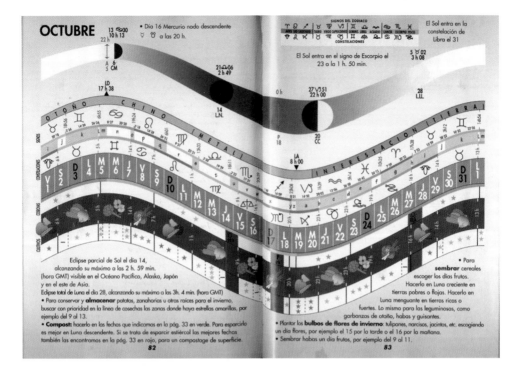

4.15 USING THE LUNAR CALENDAR

Many elderly Spaniards can remember sitting outside after dark, being instructed on the basics of astronomy and the impact of the cyclic positions of the moon, planets, constellations and the sun in relation to the earth and each other and the best timings for planting fruit and vegetables, the healthy growing of plants and the quality of their harvests.

Hearing of this, we purchased our first lunar calendar, became fascinated and tried to do likewise when we had a quiet summer evening. Unfortunately, our studies were foreshortened when street lights were installed which prevent us seeing the total night skyscape.

But the Spaniards were not the first to garden this way. Historians tell us that the Egyptians, Chinese, Celts, Greeks, Romans, Arabs and American Indians all followed a form of astronomical calendar and agriculturalists and scholarly monks continued its development in medieval Europe. Part of this knowledge was passed down generation to generation in agricultural communities.

In the early 20th century an Austrian, Rudolf Steiner, collated, extended and integrated what was then known, carried out his own research, and published his concept of the lunar solar calendar and its practical application in large-scale agriculture as well as backyard gardening in 1924. Research has continued in many parts of the world and more and more farmers and gardeners are adopting his concepts of the lunar calendar and bio-dynamic gardening, i.e. responding to the ever-changing but cyclic cosmic rhythms of the universe. Some are summarised in the table.

SOME IMPORTANT CELESTIAL CYCLES

The earth rotates off centre on its axis in relation to the moon once every 24 hours.
The moon moves elliptically around the earth every 27.2 days and affects the tides etc.
The moon orbits in relation to the planets and constellations of stars every 27 days.
The moon orbits in relation to the sun, on average, every 29.53 days, causing the phenomenon of the new and full moon cycle.
The earth moves around the sun every 365.24 days.
The Gregorian religious/social calendar adopted by the Roman Catholic world in 1582, the UK and other Protestant countries in the 1750s and by such countries as Greece and China only in the 1920s has 365 days a year plus a four-yearly leap year, a one-day adjustment to keep as close as possible to the solar cycle of 365.24 days.

Today's published agricultural/gardening calendars incorporate/interpret how all the known cause-effect relationships within the lunar-solar universe such as the impacts on the earth's electromagnetic field, temperatures, rainfalls, tides, length of night and day, gravity pulls, sun flare activity, etc. affect humans, animals, insects, birds and plants. Luckily, the end result is presented in a form easily understood by laymen gardeners like ourselves.

The chart opposite is an extract from the lunar calendar published annually in Spain by Artus Porta Manresa. We find it the easiest to follow of all the calendars we have seen and also the most comprehensive. It is normally available from November onwards in bookshops. If you have difficulties in tracing it contact calendario@lunar.infomail.es.

There is a page similar to the one illustrated for each month of the year. One does not need to be an astronomer or astrologer or understand much Spanish to use it, for everything for the amateur gardener is said in the bottom two lines of the diagram.

The four groups of vegetables - root, fruit, leaf and flower - are very obviously illustrated. The best days for doing any work on each group is indicated by three stars, the second-best days by two stars and the also-rans by one star. Days when no work should be done are indicated by the red boxes. Likewise, it is recommended that any work on fruit trees, bushes and plants is done on fruit days when the moon is at an appropriate point in its cycle. For the amateur fruit-grower the most important indicators are the three or two-star fruit days when he/she should sow seeds, plant plantlets or cuttings, graft, give extra feeds, and harvest fruits for storing or processing.

So, when we include a task in a given month in the fruit-growing calendar of Part Six, look for the best days within that month on the relevant monthly chart. Thus, our 2006 calendar suggests the following dates as best for typical tasks:

Plant new trees on November 14 and on March 13-14 when the moon is descending in the night sky.
Prune citrus trees between February 13 and 22 when the moon is waning and descending.
Spray fruit trees with neem between June 12 and 17 and between July 18 and 22.

140

Harvest walnuts for storing October 16 to 18 when the moon is waning and descending.

The wave curve of the charts indicates when the moon is rising and falling in the night sky. The clear and shaded moons on the top curve indicate the pattern of the waxing and waning moon. The lines below relate to the relationships between the planets and constellations and the moon, which are for the astrological scholars.

Bio-dynamic farming is a growing phenomenon worldwide. Bio-dynamic agriculturalists aim to do all the work on fields and greenhouses of specific groups of vegetables (root, leaf, flower and fruit) including all the tasks mentioned above, plus ploughing, hoeing, harrowing, weeding, watering, pruning extra growth and flowers, etc., on the most beneficial days according to the lunar/solar calendar. We go as far as is practical, bearing in mind that we don't work on the vegetable plot all day/every day. It would be extremely difficult to do so with a mixed plot of up to 40 vegetables compared with a commercial mono-crop field and taking into account rainy days and holidays.

The calendar is also packed with other useful easy-to-read charts. The information of most interest to the gardener includes when to cut canes, when to plant and prune fruit trees, when to spray against insects and fungi, when to best have your hair cut, etc.

4.16 HARVESTING, IMMEDIATE USE, STORING AND PROCESSING FRUITS

A few well-maintained fruit trees, bushes and plants can produce large quantities of fruit but three meals a day and snacks use them up. There are innumerable ways in which fresh, stored and healthy processed fruit can be integrated into the daily diet - and home-processed fruit does not include E colourants, flavours, sweeteners and preservatives to make them edible.

The individual fruit sections 4.2 to 4.9 have given some guidelines related to specific fruits. This section brings together some general possibilities and suggestions of what to do with the inevitable gluts.

• Eat fresh when at their best, e.g. eat your favourites as snacks, with home-made yoghurt or cream, or as a simple but wholesome dessert.

• Juice and drink fresh or freeze, e.g. oranges, mandarins, apples, pears and grapes.

• Integrate into tasty meat and fish dishes, e.g. mandarin duck, rabbits with raisins, and fish marinated in lemon juice.

• Store for a few months, e.g. melons, oranges, lemons, persimmons, apples, and pears.

• Store for a year, e.g. almonds,

walnuts, pecans and hazel nuts.

• Freeze excesses whole or sliced, e.g. raspberries, blackberries, strawberries, cherries, apricots, cranberries, blueberries and redcurrants.

• Dry excesses for energy snacks or to re-hydrate in a few months for inclusion in soups, meat and fish dishes and desserts, e.g. grapes, raspberries, strawberries, apricots, cherries, figs, papayas, mangoes, peaches, nectarines and apples.

- Salt olives dry or in brine with herbs for later eating.
- Have olives pressed at local olive press for a year's supply of extra virgin olive oil.
- Bottle in anis, brandy or rum to produce flavoursome liquors or fruit salads for Christmas and the New Year, e.g. sloes, blackberries, blueberries, peaches, apricots, cherries, prickly pear, orange or lemon rinds, mangoes, lychees, papaya, hazel nuts and walnuts.
- Produce home made wines, e.g. grapes, oranges, rhubarb, plum, blackberries, elderberries and blackcurrants.
- Prepare flavoured wines, e.g. add some slivers of lemon, mandarin or orange peel to a bottle of white wine for two days before drinking.
- Bottle in syrup for winter desserts, e.g. peaches, apricots, lychees, grapes, cherries, plums and mandarins.
- Add to bottles of apple vinegar to make flavoured vinegars for dressing salads, e.g. raspberries, redcurrants, lemons and elderberries.
- Pickle in a sweet vinegar solution for accompanying meats, e.g. tangerines, mandarins, mangoes and apples.
- Make pickles, e.g. walnuts, almonds, oranges, cherries and peaches.
- Make jams, e.g. strawberries, plums, cherries, apricots and figs.
- Make jellies for accompanying meats or cheeses, e.g. redcurrants, cranberries, and quince (*membrillo* jelly to serve with cheeses).
- Crystallise the skins for use in cooking or coating strips in chocolate for an after dinner treat, e.g. melons, oranges, lemons and papayas.
- Prepare our favourite summer dessert, a chocolate fondue, e.g. strawberries, peaches, grapes, nectarines, cherries, mangoes and papayas.

Some of the above take more time than others but the effort is worthwhile. Various stored and processed fruits can be used on a daily basis and out of season for special gastronomic occasions.

PART FIVE

PREVENTING AND CONTROLLING PROBLEMS

Problems caused by gales, fluctuating temperatures, frost, hail, snow, poor soils, drought, weeds, pests, diseases, animals and birds can all be largely prevented and controlled by simple natural, ecological and organic methods.

5.1 TREES FAIL TO BEAR FRUIT

There is nothing more frustrating than purchasing good trees, planting them carefully and then waiting for years before any fruit appears. There are several possible causes for a delay in producing fruit:

    a. The tree does not bloom. The reasons can be that:

        • The tree is not yet sufficiently mature. Most trees bear fruit by the third year but avocados can take seven years or more.

        • The flower/fruiting buds have been damaged by frost - see section 5.2. Early flowering trees are particularly vulnerable when hot spells over Christmas and in January/February stimulate trees into growth a few weeks early and then frosts occur and damage the new growth including prematurely opening buds.

        • The number of chilling hours (hours below 7 degrees Centigrade) required by many deciduous fruit trees to trigger the development of leaf and flower buds have not been achieved. This is important for the trees that do best in temperate climates (areas with cold winters but cold enough to kill trees usually grown in such areas). Typically, such fruits as apples, pears, apricots and peaches require from 500 to 1000 hours depending on the variety, nut trees over a thousand, and kiwis several hundred. Once these hours are achieved, the trees will start to spring to life whenever the weather warms up. Hence, the problem highlighted in the previous point.

146

If you plan to grow such fruits in areas where they are grown commercially, especially in Catalonia and Aragon, you will have few problems and the annual rainfalls in those areas match to a large extent their requirements. In other areas recognise that you have a challenge.

• The tree is continually stressed by being waterlogged or under-watered - see section 4.11.

• The tree is diseased or attacked by insects - see section 5.7.

• The tree has been grown from seed and is a variety that will not reproduce satisfactorily by this method. This can easily happen with citrus fruits and avocados for instance. The best thing is to graft a branch from an already fruiting tree on to the rootstock of the tree you have grown from seed - see section 4.13.

• The tree is stunted because you have inadvertently planted it over a large rock. To avoid this, when you have dug out the planting hole knock a steel rod another 50cm into the ground to check that all is soil beneath.

b. The tree blooms but does not bear fruit.

Again there are several possible causes and reasons including the following:

• The forming fruit was caught by a late frost - see section 5.2.

• Gale-force winds, driving rain or hail knocked off the blossom or young fruit. Apart from planting trees in the most sheltered part of the garden, there is not much you can do. In a large orchard the windward-side trees are likely to suffer more than most trees.

• Birds eat most of the young buds. If you see this happening place a net over the tree. Soft fruit bushes and plants are also vulnerable - see section 5.2.

• Excessive use of nitrogen-rich fertilisers added to the soil or sprayed on the foliage can result in excessive foliage growth rather than formation of blossoms and fruit.

• All fruit trees experience some fruit drop. This is nature's way of removing weak young fruits to allow the remaining ones to grow healthily and larger. But drought conditions, poor watering and feeding can result in all the fruit falling. Also, if you buy a young container-grown tree bearing fruit, this will often fall soon after planting out as the tree gives priority to the development of its essential root system. Indeed it is preferable to remove the fruit and resist forcing the tree to bear harvestable fruit the first year after planting.

• Insects attack immature fruits - see section 5.7.

• The fruit is not self-fertile and therefore requires a second tree nearby of a similar species. You need a male and female kiwi or kiwini vine within a few yards of each other and some varieties of apples, cherries and pears need similar trees around for cross-pollination. The second tree does not have to be in your garden - it could be in a neighbouring garden. If growing on a mini scale, one can plant two or three cross-pollinating dwarf fruit trees in the same planting hole to overcome the problem.

• Pollinating insects including bees may have been largely killed off by the extensive use of strong insecticides in the surrounding lands.

• Tree roots loosened by gales - see section 5.2. If it happens, firm them in again as soon as possible.

• The summer is too short and cool to fully ripen fruit. This is only likely to affect gardeners trying to grow unusual trees for the microclimate in high mountain areas of northern Spain.

5.2 PHYSICAL PROTECTION FROM THE ELEMENTS, BIRDS AND ANIMALS

A. COLD WINDS, FROSTS, SNOW AND HAIL

Although Spain generally provides a wonderful climate for growing a wide assortment of fruits, frosts, snow and severe freak hail storms do occur, not only inland and high up but down to sea level along the popular coastal strip. This may not occur every year but sufficiently often for you to be aware of the potential problems and what can be done about them.

There are five levels of potential damage:

> • Strong winds especially if accompanied by snow can cause havoc to early almond blossom.

> • An air frost a few degrees below zero can freeze flower buds just as they are about to open, which will reduce the amount of blossom and potential for forming fruit. Early-flowering trees such as almonds and apricots are the most vulnerable.
> • A similar but later frost can catch the blossom when fully out with the result that the flowers fall and no fruit forms. Vulnerable trees include almonds, apricots and citrus.

• Heavier frosts freeze the leaves of evergreen citrus trees resulting in some leaf and fruit fall.

• Very heavy frosts freeze any fruit on the trees and the inner sap of trees, resulting in branches splitting and dying back and in extreme cases trees, especially young trees, dying. The 12-year-old trees in the photograph did actually recover within a year.

The frost resistance of the various types of fruit trees, bushes and plants are indicated in the tables included in sections 4.2 to 4.9. Recognise that what matters is the temperature on the surface of the leaves. When strong winds, especially dry cold or already freezing gales, sweep through trees they cause water to evaporate from the surface cells of the leaves and the heat required to create this evaporation results in super-cooling of

the leaves. This phenomenon is termed the frost or chill factor and is what causes air frosts as opposed to ground frosts. The temperatures that can occur at various thermometer-recorded temperatures and wind speeds are indicated in the table below with an indication of typical tree tolerances.

Temperature on a thermometer (degrees C)	Wind speed in area of trees (km/hr)	Chill factor temperature on surface of leaves (degrees C)	Typical effects of chill factor temperatures on fruit trees
+2.5	0	1.5	
+2.5	8	0	Blossom can be lost at minus 2.5
+2.5	16	-5	
+2.5	24	-7.5	Tropical fruit trees are likely to be lost at minus 2.5 to 4
0	0	0	
0	8	-2.5	
0	16	-7.5	Young fruit are likely to be lost before temperatures reach minus 5
0	24	-10	
-2,5	8	-5	
-2,5	16	-10	Tips of citrus branches will be burnt at minus 5 and whole trees including the fruit by the time temperatures get down to minus 10
-2,5	24	-12.5	
-10	8	-12.5	
-10	16	-17.5	
-10	24	-25	
-15	8	-17.5	Citrus trees can be lost at minus 20, many deciduous trees by minus 30 and even olive trees at minus 40
-15	16	-25	
-15	24	-32.5	

In elevated inland areas in the more temperate north and elsewhere this occurs annually and wise gardeners don't plant fruits with low frost tolerances. However, during the winter and early spring of 2003, 2004 and 2005 exceptional air frosts lasting six to 12 hours struck on several nights from the Pyrenees to southern Andalusia. As a result considerable numbers of fruit trees were severely burned or killed in a very short space of time. In some cases the conditions were the worst experienced for 25 to 50 years.

It's any one's guess when such low temperatures could be experienced again, but a recent report suggests climatic changes over the past 30 years have resulted in spring in Spain starting two weeks earlier and autumn starting nine days later than previously. The start of spring is defined as the day when flower buds on fruit trees begin to open and the autumn by when leaves on deciduous trees in temperate areas start to fall.

The implication: longer summers will result in later new growth and less chance of this hardening off during the autumn before frosts strike, which could result in more branch ends being frost-burnt; and there is a greater chance of blossom and forming fruits being damaged by late frosts.

Actions that can be taken:

• Use frost-tolerant trees around the plot to create a wind-break for more susceptible trees further inside the garden.

• Don't plant susceptible fruits unless you are willing to accept the challenge and risk.

• Cover young trees with fleece or bubble wrap if in a frost belt or an area where frosts occasionally occur if you are risking the planting of semi-tropical fruits. In 2004 we lost a seven-year-old mango tree which the previous summer had yielded 25 large, juicy fruits that could be eaten direct from the tree. It was in front of a south-facing wall and we had covered it, as during previous winters, with three or four layers of fleece and a layer of green, woven wind-break material. Previously this had been sufficient, but it was not enough that year to resist 12 hours of well-below-zero chill factor.

Since we like mangoes and our garden is rather experimental, we have planted a new tree to see if we can achieve good crops again, 350 metres up in a valley 15 kilometres from the sea in the Valencia region.

• If you have warning of heavy frosts overnight and only have a few trees, spray them with water so that the surface water evaporates in preference to water within the cells of the leaves. You may find special sprays in your local agricultural cooperative for giving some protection from the super-cooling of leaves. It is also claimed spraying with a dilute infusion of valerian in water the evening before an expected frost can help.

• Barrels of water under fruit trees in the garden or in orchards can help, as the heat given out by water freezing can raise the ambient air temperature.

• Keep the surface of the soil under fruit trees clear of weeds and grass to increase the extent of radiated heat up into the trees from earth warmed up during the sunny days.

• If citrus trees are heavily hit, do not immediately prune damaged growth until any chance of a later frost is past. Then prune the damage. To help the trees recover, give them a foliar feed that will stimulate new growth and with luck a second flowering. The latter is unlikely to be as profuse as the regular flowering, but at least you will still have a crop that year.

· If any type of tree looks dead having lost leaf and flower buds, do not immediately cut it back or dig it out. Give it a good root and foliar feed followed by a heavy, thorough watering and leave it until the end of the summer. Trees can miraculously come back into bud and leaf after three to five months.

· The evergreen trees at most risk during winter and spring frosts are those already under shock because they have not been watered during long dry spells. Most trees will survive such conditions until the spring rains, but if the leaves are already partly dried out the effect of the surface evaporation caused by strong cold winds will worsen the situation.

· Cover soft fruits with woven netting to reduce the impact of frosts and winds.

· Cover strawberries with cloches to protect early fruits and in very exposed situations to prevent them from freezing down to the shallow roots and dying.

Every spring and summer one sees photographs in the Spanish newspapers of orchards with the trees stripped of all their leaves and fruit after a violent hail storm. Luckily, we have never experienced such a catastrophe and, if we had, there is really nothing we could do to defend ourselves against a reoccurrence (except if growing fruit commercially to take out insurance with one of the agriculturally orientated banks). Gardeners need to accept, like the Spaniards, the possibility of such an act of God and hope for the best.

Heavy snowfalls, if they thaw within a day or two, are not likely to do much damage except if freezing winds result in layers of ice on the leaves and branches. Plastic tubes around the trunks of young trees, especially citrus trees, can minimise the damage to the trunks. If young evergreen citrus trees are covered with deep snow, we suggest you brush it off with a broom to prevent the weight of snow from snapping branches.

B. GALES AND HEAVY RAINS

Gale-force winds can cause havoc to spring trees in full bloom even if it does not rain. A day or more of torrential rain can soon turn rock-hard, grey or red clay soils into a quagmire with the result that even staked trees start to tilt or fall and come out of the ground, especially if there are strong winds accompanying the rain. Heavy gales at the same time can exacerbate the problem.

The supports for trees and vines therefore need to be deeply bedded and firm. We recommend that tree support posts are knocked into the ground for 25 to 33 per cent of their length.

The posts also need to be strong and preferably long-lasting. Unfortunately, oak or chestnut posts are not readily available in all areas or are very expensive. If you use pine posts, knock them further into the ground each year to combat their inevitable rotting even

if well-treated with preservative before use. In some cases you will need to replace the posts before the roots and tree trunk are sufficiently developed to be able to do without support.

We suggest you use posts 3-4cm-thick for young trees, 6-8cm for larger trees and 10 or more for very large trees. Guy ropes or wires should be attached to larger trees to give support to the posts. Tall palm trees are a special case and are normally supported for up to three or four years by four strong, wooden struts or planks planted in deep holes in the ground and attached to the trunk of the palm with a large lump of plaster (yeso).

Do ensure that the tops of the posts are high enough to protect the entire trunk as gales can snap off trees a third of the way down due to the force of wind on the leaves and branches above the exposed trunk. Oak, chestnut or acacia posts are the strongest.

Lastly, attach the trunk of each tree to its support post with ties that will not cut into the bark.

Wide proprietary plastic and rubber straps are available or you can use a suitable length and diameter of water hose or irrigation tubing with a strong wire threaded through. Check the ties every six months to ensure that they are secure and still provide room for the trunk to thicken.

C. HOT SOUTHERLY WINDS

The only measures that can be taken are to:

    • Improve the soil before planting anything to increase its water absorbing properties. Terracotem water absorbing gel www.terravida.com mixed into the planting hole when planting trees can help.

    • Keep the soil around and between fruit trees loose to reduce capillary evaporation from the surface.

    • Plant fruit trees close so that, when mature, their branches are only 50 centimetres apart to enable the trees to keep the soil and roots in shade.

    • Fit plastic protective tubes or tapes around the trunks of young trees, especially young citrus trees.

    • Paint the trunks of fruit trees with whitewash. The white can look attractive as well as having a cooling effect.

    • Plant fruit trees through holes in black plastic sheeting, close-woven or solid, covered with 4 to 10cm of stone chippings.

    • Plant strawberries through holes in black plastic sheeting or an old carpet.

• Mulch around soft fruit bushes with compost, grass cuttings and comfrey leaves.

The other summer problem is that boughs laden with fruit can break off in high winds. It is therefore wise to support them before the fruit becomes very heavy with strong V-ended pieces of wood or pruned branches.

D. BIRDS

Some losses from birds are inevitable but, unless you attract large flocks, we suggest you live with it for the benefit of having the birds around to eat insects and the joy of having wildlife in the garden at a time when heavy, chemical spraying of fruit trees and vegetables

Plastic tube protection

takes a toll. We place scarecrows among the soft fruit - they deter new arrivals but act as a roost for the residents within a few days - and string some old CDs across the area.

If you experience serious losses, you can hang nets over trees when the fruit starts to form (e.g. with cherries and grapes), drape netting over soft fruit, plant your soft fruits within a netted fruit cage, or place bags over forming bunches of grapes or peaches.

E. WASPS

Trace and destroy nests as soon as large numbers of wasps appear and hang up traps with sugary or jammy water baits.

Wire netting and plastic tube protection

F. INSECTS (see section 5.7)

G. ANIMALS

The most troublesome are likely to be tree rats, which have a special liking for dates and almonds. As it acts like a squirrel, one may look amusing, but once its family arrives it is a different matter. Suggest you put a rat bait or a baited trap down as soon as you see one.

Real squirrels are rare and protected so accept a limited loss of fruit.

In some areas rabbits can be a pest. Place a plastic trunk guard around the trunk and a column of wire mesh around this as shown in the photograph.

Wild boar have a liking for grapes and peanuts, especially if it has been a dry summer and their drinking places have

dried up. A two-tier electric fence may inhibit them. They can also attack the bark of nut trees. The photograph shows young walnut trees protected by old oil drums.

In some areas vines are pruned so that   there are no fruiting branches less than one metre above the soil. Woven bags or wads of human hair hung on postsor wires are also useful in dete rring wild boar and rabbits, especially if the human smell is strengthened every so often with urine.

If you have a problem with deer or passing herds of sheep or goats eating the bark or lower branches of trees we suggest you erect a high fence or a two or three strand electric fence.

5.3 SUPPLEMENTARY FEEDS

The amount of nutrients required by fruit trees, bushes and plants depends on a number of factors, including:

a. Where you have planted them (see Part Three).

b. What type you have planted (see Part Four). Compact varieties and varieties grown on dwarf rooting stocks will need less nutrients than large trees.

c. The age of the trees and the extent of their spreading and deepening root systems. Young trees obviously need nutrients to grow but at the same time delicate young roots can be burned by strong chemical feeds.

d. The size of your garden and the size of trees that can be accommodated. The more you fertilise the more pruning you will have each year.

e. How well they fruit and how much fruit you require.

The various nutrients needed to help trees, bushes and plants grow healthily and productively from seedling to maturity are described below. If you have enriched your soil before planting (see sections 4.2F and 4.10), roots will be able to find and extract sufficient nutrients to expand root structures, lengthen and thicken trunks and branches and develop leaves, flowers and fruit. There is therefore no need to use supplementary feeds, organic or inorganic, until these initial reserves are depleted. This will be speedier in containers and in raised beds, where it will be necessary to start to use supplementary feeds within six months of planting up. In the open garden, supplementary feeds will not be required for several years if the soil was enriched before planting. Naturally some varieties of fruit trees are hungrier than others.

NUTRIENT NEEDS

• **Nitrogen (N)** which stimulates the developments of trunks, branches and leaves and their green colouration. But over-feeding with nitrogen fertilisers can result in excessive foliage growth at the expense of the development of flowers and fruits and the very essential root structures. Deciduous trees need nitrogen each year to develop new leaves.

• **Phosphorus (P)** in the form of phosphates which stimulate the development of strong root structures, early growth and the steady formation of mature trees, bushes and plants.

• **Potassium (K)**, often called potash, essential for the development of drought and disease resistance and the development of flower buds, flowers and fruit.

A number of minerals and trace elements are also essential for the overall health and vitality of growing trees, bushes and plants.

They are required in moderate quantities:

• **Magnesium** which helps prevent or correct the yellowing of leaves.

• **Calcium** which is essential for the development of strong cells and resistance to disease.

• **Sulphur** which helps maintain general plant health and prevent and control fungal problems.

· **Iron** which helps prevent the bleaching or blotchiness of leaves.
The main essential trace elements are as follows.
· **Zinc** which prevents leaves from developing yellow spots.
· **Manganese** which prevents the yellowing of leaves.
· **Boron, copper** and **molybdenum** which apparently contribute to the development of strong cell structures and natural disease control.

Signs that you need to apply supplementary feeds include:
· Poor development of foliage or foliage yellowing.
· Few flower buds develop.
· Few fruits develop to maturity.
· Trees remain stunted. However this may also be because you have planted over a wide slab of rock.

The normal pattern of supplementary feeds is as follows:
An emergency nitrogen and potash-rich foliar feed sprayed on trees that have lost their leaves and flowers due to frost to try to stimulate a second flowering and new leaves.
A balanced general feed in the spring when leaf and flower buds start to swell.
A feed high in potassium in early summer when fruits start to swell and mature.
Autumn feeds are not recommended as they can stimulate late new growth that can be caught by frost (see section 5.2).

There are three ways of providing the extra nutrients required.
a. Use traditional inorganic chemicals such as:
Ammonium phosphate - 20% N, 50% P.
Potassium nitrate - 15% N, 45% K.
Potassium sulphate - 50% K.
Ammonium nitrate - 30% N.
Typical mixes: for young trees, 20% N, 8% P, 8% K; for mature trees, 10% N, 18% P, 24% K.

For garden use in Spain these have some disadvantages. They are strong corrosive chemicals and one application can burn roots, especially in Spain where rainfalls are infrequent and drip irrigation systems quickly dissolve granular fast or slow-feed release fertilisers scattered on the soil into fairly concentrated liquids. Young citrus trees are especially vulnerable to root burn and rarely recover.

Leakages from bags corrode garage and shed floors. These are not things you would want children or pets to touch. Also, most gardeners are not in a position to dissolve them in tanks of water and meter them into an irrigation system as in commercial orchards.

b. Use proprietary/natural/ecological/organic liquid or solid-fertiliser products as there are now many of these "softer" and safer-to-use products available in good horticultural shops and agricultural cooperatives. Their development and marketing is driven by the increasing number of major fruit and vegetable growers in Spain who are going organic to meet the increasing demand from north European customers and to be more socially responsible with their spraying programmes.

c. It is also possible to use a number of easy-to-produce home-made natural, ecological and organic fertilisers. We mainly use these.

TYPICAL HOME-MADE FERTILISERS

Typical homemade natural supplementary feeds

Examples of why and how to use

How we prepare liquid feeds and apply dry material

Liquid comfrey made from freshly cut comfrey leaves. (1)

a. It is rich in potassium/ potash and contains significant amounts of nitrogen and phosphorous
b. It makes an excellent liquid spring fertiliser for all fruit trees, bushes or plants.

Method 1
a. Use an opaque plastic drum or barrel preferably with a tap near the base.
b. Keep in a shady place.
c. Raise up on bricks so that you can place a container under the tap.
d. Fill a large woven sack with freshly cut leaves. The sack works as a filter to stop the tap becoming clogged. This also makes it easy to remove spent leaves which can be added to the compost heap.
e. Cover with water and leave to ferment.
f. After two weeks the smelly liquid can be used as a liquid feed. Add 250ml to 5 litres of water in a watering can.

Method 2
a. If you don't have a tap, make a small hole at the base of the drum.
b. Pack the drum tightly with freshly dampened cut leaves but do not add any extra water.
c. With this method it is most important to keep the drum in the shade so the leaves stay moist and rot down.
d. Keep a container underneath the hole to collect the black liquid when it starts to drip. Add only 50ml to 5 litres of water.

Method 1 needs to be used within six months whereas method 2 will keep almost indefinitely.

Cutting comfrey

Processing comfrey

Mulching raspberries

157

TYPICAL HOME-MADE FERTILISERS

Typical homemade natural supplementary feeds	Examples of why and how to use	How we prepare liquid feeds and apply dry material
Freshly cut comfrey leaves. (See previous foto).	**a.** As a mulch around soft fruit plants **b.** Add to compost heap to enrich nutrient level.	**a.** Mix with well-rotted composts, manures and grass cuttings. **b.** Layer as in section 5.6.
Liquid nettle made from plants harvested from locations not treated with weedkillers.	**a.** It is rich in nitrogen and an excellent organic fertiliser for young trees etc. **b.** It encourages strong growth from the seedling/grafting stage and helps combat diseases and pest infestations. Once trees, bushes and plants reach fruiting stage cut back its use.	**a.** Prepare as Method 1 of Comfrey above. **b.** For a general feed use dilution of 100ml to 5 litres of water and as a foliar feed 50ml to 5 litres of water. (Nettle is very potent so always dilute well). **c.** Apply to soil or leaves. The latter especially after frost damage.
Comfrey/nettle mix	**a.** As both comfrey and nettle contain important beneficial ingredients we mix the two liquid manures to produce a combined feed. **b.** This can also be added to a liquid manure feed (see below).	Dilute as above and mix.
Liquid manure	**a.** A good general feed. **b.** As the nutrients have already been extracted, the plants can benefit immediately. **c.** Manures vary in strength: strongest, pigeon; strong, poultry, goat, sheep and a compost combining these manures and green garden and kitchen waste; medium/low, horse, cow, rabbit and composted kitchen waste.	**a.** Set up a drum or barrel as for comfrey Method 1. **b.** Place only well-decomposed manures and water in the barrels in the following quantities: strongest, I bucketful to 6 of water. strong, 1 bucketful to 4 of water. medium/low, 1 bucketful to 3 of water. The feeds will be ready for use in a couple of days. For foliar sprays dilute further 1:4 with water.
Rich well-rotted compost	**a.** A well-balanced feed for all crops especially if it contains animal and green manures such as comfrey and nettle. **b.** Always use well-decomposed compost, otherwise it will continue to decay in the soil and encourage disease and unwanted pests.	To give an extra feed, mulch plants with a thin layer of compost and hoe in lightly. Also helps to reduce water evaporation.

TYPICAL HOME-MADE FERTILISERS

Typical homemade natural supplementary feeds	Examples of why and how to use	How we prepare liquid feeds and apply dry material
Eco park compost	Composted green waste. As well as containing important nutrients for growing all types of fruit, it adds beneficial humus to the soil.	Mulch around plants helps to add extra nutrients, retain moisture and keep the soil light and workable.
Eco park compost including seaweed	As above, but also good for lightening heavy soils due to its general compost and sand content.	Mulch around plants helps to add nutrients, retain moisture and keep the soil light and workable.
Wood ash	**a.** Produced by burning mature wood it is high in minerals especially potash. Bonfires with other green materials are of lesser value. **b.** We use it for feeding soft fruits as it encourages healthy strong roots.	**a.** Collect and keep in a dry place until needed as once it gets wet the minerals leach out. **b.** Sprinkle around base of plants. **c.** It will add valuable nutrients to the compost heap if sprinkled over the various layers.
Chicken manure	**a.** Contains many plant nutrients but most of all nitrogen which is beneficial to young trees, bushes and plants. **b.** Can also be used as a liquid manure (see above).	**a.** Manure from chickens kept under cover in our area is usually a mixture of left-over grains and their bedding of rice husks so it needs to be left for at least a year to rot down before use. **b.** Alternatively, collect dried droppings from your own hens, beat them to a fine powder, mix 2x1 with fine soil or wood ash and spread finely around the drip line of trees in the spring.
Bone meal	**a.** A good natural general slow-release fertiliser. **b.** Use it less than before coming to Spain as we have all the above alternatives.	Sprinkle over soil once a year.
Blood	More readily available in powder form (Sequestrene) than in liquid. Excellent for correcting yellowing of leaves. Use a dilute liquid feed as the fruits start to form.	

TYPICAL HOME-MADE FERTILISERS

Typical homemade natural supplementary feeds	Examples of why and how to use	How we prepare liquid feeds and apply dry material
Dried neem cake (2)	Residue left after neem kernels and seeds are crushed to extract neem oil, used as an insecticide.	**a.** Apply as for bone meal. **b.** Also helps control slugs around strawberries and snails on citrus trees.
Banana skins * and spent leaves**	* High in potassium. ** High in nitrogen.	Cut up and mulch around base of plants.
Orchard weeds including the bright yellow-flowered Oxalis pes-caprae found around the countryside and in many gardens in spring	Useful mix of nutrients.	Rotavate into soil in autumn and spring (see section 5.4)

Notes:

(1) Comfrey *(consuelda)* is a herb that is invaluable in the organic growing of both fruit and vegetables. It can easily be grown as a line or patch in the orchard, a corner of the garden or around the vegetable patch. The best variety to use is comfrey symphytum-x-uplandicum, otherwise known as Bocking 14 Russian comfrey.

Unlike other varieties it rarely self-seeds. You only need a few root cuttings to start as they grow fast and can be split each November or March to provide new plants. Our original seven small cuttings have now become several hundred plants surrounding our vegetable plot. Cuttings should be planted in rows or blocks 30cm apart. The only requirement is that the roots are kept damp and fed with a spring nitrogen feed (we use chicken manure) from time to time. Comfrey leaves are rich in potassium and also contain good sources of nitrogen, phosphorus and trace elements. The comfrey roots go very deep to extract these nutrients from the sub-soil which the roots of most vegetable plants don't reach. In Spain comfrey plants will normally die back between December and the end of February. In most situations the leaves can be harvested by cutting them three to five times a year. If you have difficulty in obtaining comfrey plants locally in Spain, you can purchase them by mail order from the following suppliers: www.OrganicCatalogue.com, www.edwintucker.com, comfreyplants@hotmail.com and www.chilternseeds.co.uk.

(2) Neem cake is what is left after neem seeds are cold-pressed. It can be sprinkled on the soil around vegetable plants or mixed into seed beds to give some protection against insects and slugs as well as acting as a slow-release general fertiliser. The cake can be obtained in Spain from Trabe (www.trabe.net) and from Germany from Niem-Handel (kontact@niem-handel.de or www.niem-handel.de).

5.4 WORKING THE SOIL

Guidelines for planting fruit trees, bushes and plants have been given in previous sections. This section provides guidelines for general soil management around established trees, bushes and plants to ensure healthy conditions are maintained.

It is important to work the top 5cm of the soil under and around fruit trees to prevent compacting, minimise water evaporation and the harbouring of pests in any grass and weed cover, and enable rain, irrigation water and fertilisers to penetrate the soil so they are extracted by the tree roots rather than vigorous weeds. Also the removal of plant growth under trees during the winter ensures the maximum heating of the soil during sunny days and the maximum radiant heat up into the trees at night, which can give some protection should a night frost occur.

There are four possible approaches to weed control, each with their benefits and risks.

    a. Rotavate the ground around the trees each spring and autumn to a depth of 5cm to:

        • Loosen the compacted surface and work the surface grass and weeds into the soil to add nutrients and improve the moisture-holding capacity of the soil. This is very important if you have the bright yellow flowered *Oxalis pes-caprae* growing un-

161

der your fruit trees. Although this South African weed entered Spain by mistake, it is regularly seen as a spring carpet in orange groves and orchards and has become an important source of soil nutrients.

• Bury and kill any pests lurking in the grass.
• Bury any decaying remains of fallen fruit.

All that is positive, but there is the danger of damaging shallow roots so rotavate no more than 5cm deep and keep a metre away from tree trunks. Weed the last metre by hand or by careful hoeing. Excess rotavating can also damage the soil structure and build up an impermeable layer in poor soils just below the depth of the blades.

Before and after rotavating

b. Weed-kill the orchard once or twice a year to kill all the grass and wild flowers. As that does not remove the pests feeding on leaves and fallen fruit, you will need to add an insecticide to your weed-killing spray. Altogether, not an ecologically friendly approach.

c. Mulch deeply around the trees with well-rotted compost to inhibit the growth of grass and weeds and reduce moisture evaporation from the soil. However, pests may be attracted and breed in the humid microclimate of the compost and fungal diseases may attack the base of tree trunks. Therefore mulch in the autumn and rotavate the mulch into the soil well before the trees bud or in the case of citrus fruits flower. Again do not rotavate more than 5cm deep. Also a dry mulch can prevent light rain from reaching the surface of the soil as all is absorbed by the mulch.

d. Cover the area around the fruit trees with woven, black plastic sheeting and cover with 5cm of stone chippings except for a half-metre-diameter circle around the trunk of each fruit tree. This will keep tidy the area around individual specimen fruit trees anywhere in the garden or dedicated orchard areas as the chippings will inhibit weed growth. An additional benefit is that there will be a significant reduction in the amount of water evaporated during hot and windy weather. However fallen leaves and fruit will need to be cleared as soon as they build up to prevent pests and diseases as well as keeping the areas looking tidy.

e. Whichever approach you take, it is worth spraying the ground under fruit trees in the autumn and spring with neem (see section 5.7).

5.5 CONTROLLING THE WEEDS

Wherever you grow your fruit and whether you grow them inorganically or organically, some weeds are inevitable. While weed growth in orchards can be usefully worked into the soil twice a year to produce a slow low-level feed, this is not possible except with a very narrow rotavator if growing in strip beds, around the vegetable plot or in raised beds, and is definitely out if trees are planted within the general garden and in containers.

If you are growing organically, weed-killers are out except for a 3-to-5-per-cent solution of vinegar and even that can kill some valuable micro organisms in the soil and worms working the surface layers of the soil. Also in many areas around villages, where channelled water is used for the irrigation of fields and allotments of fruit and vegetables, weed-killers are not allowed past a certain date each spring related to when persons start to irrigate using the open channels.

So what can be done? The best thing is to weed as you would the rest of the garden on a monthly basis and compost the weeds along with fallen fruit and leaves as outlined in section 5.6, except for deep-rooted perennial weeds with seed heads which are best burnt.

Monthly should be frequent enough even for the strawberry bed and around currant bushes and vines.

Within orchards all weeds can be rotavated into the top 5 to 10cm of the soil to provide a green manure. Over the years this will enrich the upper layers of the soil from which rainfall and irrigation will flush nutrients down to the roots.

If you have a sizeable orchard of mature trees, one or two sheep will be sufficient to keep the weeds cropped and their droppings will also add nutrients to the soil. Unfortunately sheep might feed on young trees. A strimmer is an alternative.

Remember that weeding is done not only for tidiness but also to stop unwanted plants from using up valuable nutrients and moisture especially during the hotter months and to keep the soil aerated.

However, if you live in a country area and like to live off the land, collecting wild blackberries, sloes, wild mushrooms and asparagus, recognise that some wind-blown and bird-seeded weeds have a number of valuable uses beyond the compost heap, as outlined in the following table.

163

TABLE - USEFUL USES OF TRADITIONAL WEEDS

WEED	Adds taste to salads	Makes tasty soups	Steamed as a tasty tapas or vegetable	Boiled with potatoes as tasty tapas or vegetable	Fried as tapas or vegetable
Wild asparagus	•	•	•		•
Wild rocket	•				
Dandelion	•				
Chicory	•		•		
Fennel	•	•	•	•	
Borage			•		
Poppy			•	•	
Horsetail					
Nettles		•			
Wild Garlic	•	•	•		•

Note: Use the young leaves in all cases, except for wild asparagus where you eat the young stems. You can use the stems and corms of wild garlic.

5.6 COMPOSTING WEEDS AND FRUIT WASTE FOR RECYCLING TO THE SOIL

WHY COMPOST WHEN GROWING FRUIT

As explained in Part Four, and section 5.3 compost is invaluable in:

a. Mixing into the soil before planting fruit trees, bushes and plants to improve nutrient content, the lightness to enable roots to more easily search out nutrients and moisture, moisture-absorbing properties and drainage. This applies to those planted in all types of containers as well as in the ground.

b. For mulching around the base of soft fruit bushes and plants to ensure they do not dry out and to provide nutrients.

c. Making up composts when growing strawberries and some fruit trees from seed, other soft fruits and some fruit trees from cuttings.

d. Obtaining liquid manures for feeding window boxes, containers and the garden.

Good rabbit food	Add to compost heap	Steeped in water for use as a liquid fertiliser	Infused in water for insect deterrent or fungicide
•	•		
•	•		
•	•		
	•		
	•		
	•		
			• (F)
		•	• (ID)

WHAT IS A GOOD COMPOST?

A sweet-smelling loamy soil rich in water retaining humus, plant nutrients, beneficial micro organisms and a worm population produced by the natural aerobic decomposition of green kitchen and garden waste.

WHEN AND FROM WHAT CAN IT BE MADE?

At any time of the year from daily fruit and vegetable kitchen waste, fallen leaves from fruit trees, shredded prunings from fruit trees and all other trees in the general garden, weeds and fallen fruit (the only things that need to be limited are fallen citrus fruits and skins from the kitchen which can raise the acidity of the finished compost). Old newspapers are also useful additions, as will be explained later.

We do not compost meat or fish waste as it can smell, can add non-beneficial bacteria, and attract insects and rodents.

WHY BOTHER?

There are several benefits, even for the small-scale fruit-grower.

a. It is a convenient ecological way of recycling green waste back into the soil, especially the daily kitchen waste and the many sacks of shredded material that result from each year's pruning.

b. Small, enclosed, tidy, largely odourless composters are now commercially available

165

so that even apartment-dwellers can compost their daily kitchen waste and the droppings from the canary cage.

c. It reduces the municipal costs for disposing of household and garden waste and reduces the number of plastic bags used.

d. You can produce a less expensive and better-quality compost than many commercial brands or the compost produced by municipal eco parks.

WHAT TYPES OF COMPOSTERS CAN BE USED?

Good compost can be made in a number of types of composters, both purchased proprietary and home-made. The most commonly used ones are described in the table opposite.

Wiggly Wigglers mini composter

Smaller composters are available that can be hung on the walls of apartment terraces. Some local authorities supply them in the UK.

Wormeries nos. 1, 2 and 4 are easy to keep provided you don't overload them and don't let the composting material become too wet or acid.

Composters of type no.3 give few problems provided you use the recommended accelerators.

Enclosed, plastic-lidded composters of type no.5 are tidy and work best if some garden waste is mixed in with kitchen waste. Compost accelerators can speed the process. Bottom doors make removal of finished compost easy.

Rotary and tumbler composters of type no. 7 work most productively if they are filled with a mix of dry and moist material and are turned regularly. Said to be good for grass cuttings. Best if compost accelerators are added.

The box-type composters nos. 6, 8 and 9, whether purchased or home-made, are the best means of composting large amounts of shredded garden waste. They do need some

TYPE OF COMPOSTER	Capacity for adding material for composting	Speed of composting process	Cleanliness	Cost to purchase or make and in time expand	Ease of expansion without buying a second unit
1. Proprietary wormery e.g. Wiggly Wigglers' worm factory**	Small	High	High	Medium	Low
2. Home made wormery using old glass fibre water tank	Small to medium	Medium to high	Medium to high	Low	High, just find another tank
3. Small proprietary composting bins e.g Bokashi composter**	Very small	High	High	Medium	Low
4. Multi trayed composter with large worm population e.g. Wiggly Wigglers. 'Can-O-Worms'unit**	Medium	High	High	Medium	Low
5. Plastic-lidded composting bins as issued by some local councils free or at a subsidised price	Medium	Medium	High	Low/medium	Low
6. Proprietary wooden or plastic solid-sided composting boxes	Medium to large	Medium	Medium/high	Medium/high	Low
7. Proprietary rotary or tumbler composters of various designs.	Medium	High to very high	High	Medium to very high	Low
8. Home-made wire mesh and four-post composting box	Medium to large	Medium	Medium	Low/medium	High with little cost
9. Home-made from old wooden pallets or doors with wire-mesh front	Medium to large	Medium	Medium	Low	High with little cost
10. Dug out composting pit covered with soil or a tarpaulin	Medium to large	Low to medium	Medium to low	Low	High with little cost
11. Pile of material above ground covered with tarpaulin or thick black plastic	Medium to very large	Low to medium	Medium	Low	High with little cost

**Supplied by Wiggly Wigglers (www.wigglywigglers.co.uk). This not only provides a supply of good compost but also a strong liquid manure can be run off through the tap at the bottom.

special attention in Spain due to the generally dry climate. We therefore outline below the procedure found to work best and now used on a line of five home-made compost boxes.

Pits like no. 10 can work but the hole needs digging out and also the finished compost. Box composters are easier to work and extend.

Compost piles no.11 do not compost well in Spain due to the dry climate.

Clodagh merrily preparing compost heap!

LOCATION OF COMPOST HEAPS

As near as possible to the main source of materials to be composted and where it will be used. If you have a large garden, it might therefore make sense to compost near the vegetable plot and/or near the orchard. Also, if possible, locate your compost-making unit in the shade of a tree to reduce moisture evaporation during the summer.

THE SUCCESS FACTORS FOR COMPOST BOXES

Whether you use compost bins, or have just a heap in a corner in the garden, all will eventually rot down with the help of heat, moisture, oxygen, micro organisms, insects and worms. In theory you can just let nature take its course, but there are a few tricks of the trade, especially in the Spanish climate.

Factors which we have found contribute to the making of a good compost, speedily and hygienically, include:

1. The design of the composting boxes

Proprietary bins or well-operated boxes are essential here in Spain, as the open compost heap many gardeners use in rainy northern Europe would soon dry out in the hot Mediterranean climate.

We therefore suggest you construct two or three composting boxes of the following dimensions: width, depth and height a minimum of one to one-and-a-half metres as it is difficult to build up essential heat at the heart of smaller boxes. Two boxes are better than one as during the process of composting the decomposing material needs to be turned. A third box allows you to start a second heap as well as providing a spare box for turning.

A home-made box can be easily constructed by using four posts and wire netting or three old pallets. The front is most easily closed with a wire netting gate or removable wooden slats for ease of access. To increase aeration use as the base either a 10 or 15cm layer of broken twigs or a fourth pallet. It is best not to place the frame on a concrete base as you need to encourage small insects, worms and micro organisms from the soil into the heap.

2. Positioning of compost boxes

The compost heap needs to retain moisture and build up heat. Ideally, it should be situated in a semi-shaded corner of the garden.

3. Lining and covering

To retain moisture and internal heat, line your box with cardboard from old cartons or thick layers of newspaper as you build up the waste materials. Don't make air holes as you would have done in northern Europe as this will only result in the rapid drying-out of the outer layers. Keep the top covered with a layer of damp newspapers topped with a square of old carpet.

4. Layering the different raw materials

Don't just throw the waste materials into the bin willy-nilly. If you do, the decomposition will be patchy and essential heat will not build up. Build the heap layer by layer as follows:

a. Start with a 15cm layer of coarse twiggy material to create air circulation and help start the aerobic decomposition process.

b. 10-15cm of manure or half-decomposed compost. This will attract worms and essential micro organisms.

c. 10-15cm of green waste.

d. 10-15cm of brown waste.

e. four sheets of wet newspaper laid over the top. Worms love it, but avoid colour-printed pages as they may be toxic.

f. 10-15cm of manure.

g. A sprinkling of wood ash.

Repeat (c) to (g) adding natural accelerators (discussed below) to the layers until the compost box is full.

5. A good mix of raw materials, including:

· **Green waste** - vegetables, fruit peelings and fallen or unused whole fruits (limit the amount of citrus fruits or skins as they are too acidic), crushed egg shells, weeds, soft green cuttings and prunings, grass cuttings, non-diseased leaves and stems of vegetables that have finished cropping, dampened and torn-up paper packets, newspapers, cardboard in centre of toilet rolls and kitchen towel rolls. Don't use cooked kitchen waste, cheese, oil or raw meat, fish, etc. as it may attract vermin and flies in the height of summer.

• **Brown waste** - dry fibrous materials such as shredded hard prunings and branches, cuttings, flower heads, stalks, dry leaves, waste from a vacuum-cleaner, animal and human hair. It is preferable not to add cuttings from bay, conifers, acacias and oleanders as their residues can be toxic to other plants.

• **Wood ash -** a little will add valuable potassium and lime.

• **Manures -** horse, sheep, goat, rabbit, chicken and pigeon. Stack the latter two to rot down separately as they are very strong, and then only add in small proportions.

• **Accelerators -** seaweed, comfrey, borage, dandelion and nettle in leaf or liquid form are all good accelerators, also adding essential nutrients to the heap. The liquid forms can be prepared by steeping leaves in water for two or more weeks. If you don't have access to any of the above, use sulphate of ammonia or a proprietary powder. Human urine is also very effective!

• **Water -** essential to the whole process.

5. Moisture control

Dampen each layer, where necessary, as you build up the heap. This is the best time to add your prepared liquid accelerators. There is no point in leaving material dry as it won't rot down. But don't over-soak as it will then become slimy, stick together and smell as anaerobic rather than aerobic decomposition will start. It is just a matter of trial and error.

6. Temperature control/decomposition

It is important to line and cover the heap to build up the temperature necessary for bacterial action. Ideally the centre will reach 50 to 60 degrees C so as to kill off weed seeds, etc. It will decompose at lower temperatures, but at a slower rate.

Two forms of decomposition can occur within a compost heap.

• **Aerobic.** Fast, requiring oxygen. If the heap is well-mixed with dampened materials, it will fully decompose in six to 12 months.

• **Anaerobic.** Slower and smellier. Material in the heap often becomes slimy and compacted as a result of being over-wet. The solution: turn the heap while layering in new dry material. The aim is to achieve a totally aerobic process, but even in the best there will be odd corners of anaerobic decomposition taking place.

7. Turning

It is advisable to turn your heap after four to six months to re-aerate it. Prepare an empty bin as if starting a heap. Fork over the decomposing heap to the empty bin, mixing any dry materials on the outer edge into wet compost in the centre. Remove the lower part if it is ready to use. It should be fine and sweet-smelling.

At this stage you top up the partially composted material with fresh materials, and then repeat the process in four to six months' time. Label the date it was turned.

8. Worms

Worms play an important role in the compost heap. They eat damp waste material and excrete processed waste as very fertile worm castes, and their burrows aerate the heap. They will be attracted by the heat and dampness, but do add in any you find around the garden and always put back any found in the finished compost. They will leave the compost if it is too dry.

9. Potential problems and solutions

Rats - don't include any raw or cooked meat, fish, cheese, oil or salads dressed in oil.

Flies - always top kitchen waste with a layer of dry materials and cover. If they do become a problem, use a fly trap which uses a non-smelly bait.

Ants - in a drying heap ants will look for moisture in the form of retreating worms. Your worm population is valuable so find where the ants are coming from and put down ant powder or sprinkle sulphur around the base.

10. Be patient

One is always short of compost in the fruit and vegetable gardens. But don't try to take a shortcut by using the heap before it is fully decomposed, unless you are using it only for mulching or preparing bean and pumpkin trenches.

Our approach to composting in a hot dry climate is based on many years of trial and error. Yes, it does take time, but just think of the end result. All that lovely, inexpensive, fine loam and the fact that you have made the best use of your garden and household rubbish, as well as helping the environment. Each time you eat your daily fresh fruit think of your contribution to reducing the size of the local tip, the use of chemicals and the need to cut down more of the Brazilian and African palm forests to produce compost for gardeners.

5.7 ECO CONTROL OF PESTS AND DISEASES

A. GENERAL GUIDELINES

1. In general trees, bushes and plants grown in well-prepared enriched soil, watered moderately and not near diseased trees are those most likely to grow naturally and healthily. If you achieve this, the rest of this section will need to be referred to only occasionally. But - if you do not enrich the soil before planting, you force trees, bushes and plants into faster, weak growth by excessive watering and feeding and your garden is surrounded by abandoned orchards full of diseased fruit trees - this section may become the one you refer to most frequently in the entire book.

2. Plant fruit that is normally grown in your area or ensure that you provide more sheltered conditions for the more tender varieties. Trees that experience unusually hot dry summers or winter frosts for their variety can have weakened growth and will be more susceptible to diseases and plagues.

3. When considering buying fruit trees, bushes or plants, check whether virus-free varieties are available and do not purchase any with visible pests or diseases.

4. Recognise that some fruits give more problems than others. Figs, persimmons, almonds, cherries, olives and strawberries normally have few problems compared with apples, pears, peaches. Kiwis have fewer problems if grown in a cooler wetter climate such as in Galicia.

5. Intense cultivation in closely planted orchards can create more problems than individual trees within or surrounding the flower and vegetable garden as viruses and degenerative diseases can spread from tree to tree.

6. Ensure that fallen fruit, especially if rotting, is raked up from under trees otherwise it can be a breeding ground for pests, although obviously this does not always happen.

7. Fungal diseases and insect plagues can occur when fruit trees are over-watered or the land becomes water-logged after rain and/or the trees are over-fertilised with nitrogenous fertilisers. It is preferable that the land slopes a few degrees to allow excess water to run off. Also slope the earth upwards towards trunks and keep any mulching away from the trunks (see section 5.2).

8. Recognise that pest problems can be caused by chemical spraying which kills off beneficial insects, birds and small animals that are the natural predators of harmful insects. This may occur due to the spraying of surrounding orchards and vegetable-growing areas and not only by your own spraying. So we recommend that you develop a natural ecological garden including the orchard. If you stop using chemical sprays, more natural predators will soon reappear. This can be accelerated and intensified by putting up nesting boxes and companion planting plants that attract the natural predators. An area of wild flowers, herbs such as fennel, rue, dill and coriander, alfalfa or even nettles within or around an orchard can be of great benefit as can a small pond. Birds, bats, geckos, frogs, toads, ants, ladybirds and other predator insects can make a surprising comeback if you encourage them.

9. Winter mineral oil sprays can be useful preventative measures, but many should not be sprayed once there is any sign of buds swelling in the late winter. Neem, a light fruit oil, can be sprayed at any time of year. Its use is explained later.

10. Don't mulch under any tree or plant with diseased leaves. Always burn them rather than putting them on the compost heap.

11. A natural chemical-free orchard is important if the area is to be regularly used by the family, especially children, as a shady leisure area.

12. Serious infestations are less likely to occur if you plant several types of fruit rather than an orchard with a single type of fruit. There will be lower concentrations of specific harmful insects and, if you follow the above recommendations, there will be more natural predators to feed on them.

13. If you have a large orchard in a commercial fruit-growing area where programmed chemical spraying from the ground or air is the norm, you will probably need to do likewise as few natural predators will make it to your land. But do try and use ecological/biological natural products.

14. If you do need to resort to seasonal spraying against the citrus minador, do use ecological/biological sprays. In the tables that follow we indicate what can be made up at home or purchased commercially.

15. If you do use hazardous sprays, ensure you wear a face mask, rubber gloves and rubber boots as well as long-sleeved clothing. As agriculturalists become more safety-conscious, "space suit" sprayers are becoming a regular feature of rural Spain. But there is not always a warning flag and the spraying is not always stopped when one walks by. If you have to spray near a road, please be more socially responsible even when cars go by. The windows may be open.

16. Year by year more and more ecological/natural/organic insecticides and fungicides are becoming available that are less toxic to human beings, animals and beneficial insects than previous generations of products. We do not provide a list of all the current products as they are constantly changing due to scientific developments and the fact that sometimes insects become immune to the active ingredients in existing insecticides, which prompts the manufacturers to change their composition. In the table below we describe the most common problems you might experience with a wide range of fruit trees, bushes and plants and suggest some practical solutions.

If in doubt about the nature of any plague or disease in your garden, cut a piece off, seal it in a plastic bag and take it to your nearest horticultural shop or agricultural cooperative.

We do not guarantee that the solutions we offer are 100 per cent effective or as fast as some stronger toxic products, but they do go a long way to solving problems safely. In general, we believe that most gardeners are willing to accept that some fruit and leaves will always be affected whatever one does.

17. Research is under way to produce cost-effective live natural predators or plague insects that have been genetically modified for release in orchards. If you're lucky your local agricultural cooperative can already obtain a supply of these for coping with a major minador infestation on citrus trees or aphids on fruit trees. One of the best predators for aphids is ladybirds. They can be obtained by mail order from www.organiccatalogue.com.

18. Don't spray on windy days as the drift will fall on other plants, animals, birds and people - including possibly your neighbours enjoying an al fresco dinner.

19. If possible, spray with insecticides in the early morning as insects are most active during the day and employ fungicides in the evening as fungi tend to develop during the more humid night conditions.

20. Purchase a collection of small and medium-sized hand sprayers and an easily carried back-pack sprayer.

SOME COMMON PESTS, DISEASES AND ECOLOGICAL, NATURAL AND ORGANIC SOLUTIONS

DISEASE OR PEST	Typical fruits attacked	What to watch out for	Suggested solutions to choose from

A. INSECTS, BIRDS AND ANIMALS

DISEASE OR PEST	Typical fruits attacked	What to watch out for	Suggested solutions to choose from
APHIDS Aphidius/*pulgones*	Citrus, apple, almonds, apricots and pear	Leafed branches of trees and buds look dehydrated. Might also be a fine sticky film over everything	* Spray with potassium soap* or neem oil.**
BIRDS *Pájaros*	Redcurrants	Birds eating fruit buds and bunches thinned.	* Cover with fruit cage or netting.
	Strawberries	Holes in fruit	
	Fruit trees	Birds eating fruit buds	* Hang bird-scarers in trees. * Cover dwarf trees with nets.
	Grapes	Birds eating fruit	* Hang protective nets over bunches.
CODLING MOTH *Carpocapsa*	Pip fruits such as apples and pears Also affects nuts such as walnuts and almonds	Moths around trees, excreta around hole in fruit and grubs inside. Small hole in shell but often don't find until you open	* Traps in trees. * Fit grease bands in autumn. * Spray in winter and spring with neem oil or proprietary winter oil wash.
LEAF CURL *Abolladora/lepra*	Peaches, nectarines and cherries	Blistering curled-up leaves	* Preventive spraying with decoction of horsetail, nettle and bird droppings in late winter and early spring before leaf buds open. * Plant a clove of garlic at base of all trees. * Spray with copper sulphate - but this is not strictly organic. * If problem still arises, remove as many affected leaves as possible and then spray decoction as above. * Clean up fallen leaves. * Give tree a high-in-nitrogen foliar * feed (see section 5.3).
MEALY BUGS/ WOOLY APHIDS *Cochinillas*	Citrus fruits and apples	Sticky white blotches on branches covering aphids, and ants going up trunk to feed	* Scrub off where possible with an old tooth brush and a potassium soap solution or brush with alcohol of mentholated spirit. * Spray with strong jet of potassium soap solution * or beer.

175

SOME COMMON PESTS, DISEASES AND ECOLOGICAL, NATURAL AND ORGANIC SOLUTIONS

DISEASE OR PEST	Typical fruits attacked	What to watch out for	Suggested solutions to choose from
A INSECTS, BIRDS AND ANIMALS			
MEDITERRANEAN FRUIT FLIES/MOTHS *Mosca de la fruta, lepidopteros, zeuzero, hoplo-campa*	Stone and pip fruits, including plums, pears, apples, olives, and citrus	Leaf curl Young fruit falling off Maturing fruit with small holes in flesh and excreta around hole, grubs inside fruit	* Spray preventively fortnightly in autumn, winter and spring (pre and post-flowering) and summer with neem or another light oil wash or potassium soap solution. * Spray with Rotenone, a chrysanthemum-based insecticide. * For a ready available spray use a solution of potassium soap or an ecological washing-up liquid. * Clean up fallen fruit and do not put on compost heap. * Grease or glue bands around trunks during winter and spring. * Fresh traps hanging in trees throughout the year.
	Blueberries	Maggots in fruit	* Spray as above. * Mulch under plants with straw.
VINEGAR FLIES *Mosca vinagre*	Fleshy stone and pip fruits	Small gnat-like flies feeding on fermenting fallen fruit	* Clean up fallen fruit. * Spray soil and under-growth around trees with neem, nettle or potassium soap solution in spring and summer.
CITRUS LEAF MINER *Minador de cítricos*	Citrus	Curling of leaves and small holes in leaves followed by hardening of branch	* Encourage predators. * Set free neutered moths. * Hang moth traps on trees throughout the year. * Spray in Feb/Mar and Oct/Nov with a neem nettle mix*** or the latest recom-mended ecological insecti-cide. * Cut out affected leaves
PROCESSIONARY CATERPILLARS *Procesionaria del pino*	Pine nut tree (Pino pinea)	White silky nests formed around needles enclosing caterpillars or processio-ns of caterpillars on the ground in late winter/early spring	* If nests can be reached on foot or by ladder, cut off carefully into a plastic bag, seal and burn. * If the caterpillars are on the ground, do not touch by hand. The best solution is to burn them safely.****

DISEASE OR PEST	Typical fruits attacked	What to watch out for	Suggested solutions to choose from

A. INSECTS, BIRDS AND ANIMALS

DISEASE OR PEST	Typical fruits attacked	What to watch out for	Suggested solutions to choose from
RABBITS *Conejos*	Young trees	Bark stripped off and low branches eaten	* Place plastic tube guards and wire netting around trunks. * Place bags of human hair on canes near young trees.
RED BEETLE (LONG NOSED) *Picudo rojo*	Date palms	Signs of beetle activity and centre of the crown of tree dying	* Contact local *Medio Ambiente* Department and report that you have a *Rhwnchophorus ferrugineus* problem. * Arrange felling and burning. * Avoid buying imported palms.
RED SPIDER MITE *Acaro*	Citrus and apricots	Speckled leaves and leaf fall	* Spray with potassium soap solution. *Could also try neem.
SCALE *Escama*	Citrus	Hard black scales on bark	* Use toothbrush with potassium soap solution and scrub off where possible. * Spray with neem oil in autumn/winter. * Spray with potassium soap solution.
SLUGS AND SNAILS *Babosas y caracoles*	Raspberries, strawberries and redcurrants	Presence and signs of fruit being eaten	* Remove by hand. * Place beer traps by/among plants. * Surround bed by line of gritty sand, prickly oak leaves, pine leaves, comfrey leaves or crushed neem seeds. * Spray along bottom of raspberry canes and around strawberries with garlic solution. * Slug pellets as last resort
	Citrus trees and kiwis,etc.	Presence and young leaves being eaten.	* Be vigilant, remove large edible snails by hand, put in cage and feed with rosemary twigs for a month before using for a snail dish. * Place beer traps under trees. * Slug pellets as last resort. Buy Eco pellets if possible.

177

SOME COMMON PESTS, DISEASES AND ECOLOGICAL, NATURAL AND ORGANIC SOLUTIONS

DISEASE OR PEST	Typical fruits attacked	What to watch out for	Suggested solutions to choose from
A. INSECTS, BIRDS AND ANIMALS			
WASPS *Avispas*	Stone fruits at ripening time	Wasps around trees and feeding on ripest fruit	* Wasp traps - bowls of soapy water, jam jars with jam and water which they drown in. * Find and destroy nests with care. * Clear up fallen fruit.
WILD BOAR *Jabalí*	Grapevines	Low bunches of grapes eaten	* Install two-wire electric fence. * Change from bush to espalier vines. * Hang muslin bags filled with human hair at ends of rows. * Urinate daily around the vineyard!
	Peanuts	Signs of digging	* As above, except for second point.
B. FUNGAL DISEASES			
SOOTY LEAVES *La negrilla*	Citrus, often as a follow-up to mealy bug	Leaves covered in fine sooty deposit which stops photosynthesis	* Spray with potassium soap, horsetail or neem. May need several treatments to eradicate. * If the tree is small, clean leaves with toothbrush with potassium and horsetail solution.
CORAL SPOT *Necrosis de las ramas*	Raspberries, redcurrants and blackcurrants	Branches dying back and orange spots on dead wood	* Cut out and burn. * Spray bush with horsetail infusion or a proprietary fungicide.
POWDERY MILDEW *Mildiu/oidio*	Apples, pears, quince and vines, etc	White coating on leaves, branches and fruit	* Plant resistant varieties. * Dust vines lightly with sulphur fortnightly. * Spray with proprietary fungicide or horsetail infusion fortnightly. * Cut out serious infections and burn.
	Strawberries	White coating on leaves and fruit	* Dust leaves with sulphur or spray with horsetail infusion if it occurs. * Don't wet leaves when watering.

DISEASE OR PEST	Typical fruits attacked	What to watch out for	Suggested solutions to choose from

B. FUNGAL DISEASES

DISEASE OR PEST	Typical fruits attacked	What to watch out for	Suggested solutions to choose from
POWDERY MILDEW *Mildiu/oidio*	Bananas	Leaves curl up and become covered with white mould	* Spray with proprietary fungicide or horsetail infusion. * Don't use affected banana leaves as a mulch around banana plants.
BOTRYTIS *Botritis*	Strawberries	Fruit going browny-grey as covered with fungal growth and eventually rotting Whole plants rotting off	* Place mats around stems of plants or plant through black plastic. * Place straw under leaves and fruit. * Avoid wetting plants when watering. * If growing under cloches keep them ventilated. * Spray with horsetail infusion or proprietary fungicide. * Remove affected fruit or plants, don't put on compost heap.
FUNGI *Hongos*	Any fruit tree at soil level	Bark splitting or signs of fungus	* Cut off loose bark and diseased branches, then spray well with a fungicide or nettle or horsetail infusion. * Seal damaged area with pruning sealer. * Keep soil around trunks free of manures, herbage and rotting fruit. * Always clear up fallen fruit. * Make watering circle as a moat, keeping soil around trunk as an "island" above the highest water line to prevent trunk becoming water-logged.
	Grape vines and kiwi fruit	Withering/rotting of branches and fruit	* Prune affected parts and burn. * Dust vines from February to April fortnightly with sulphur powder shaken through an old sock or stocking. * If it rains when grapes are at final swelling and changing colour, they are very vulnerable. Spray with dilute copper sulphate.

179

SOME COMMON PESTS, DISEASES AND ECOLOGICAL, NATURAL AND ORGANIC SOLUTIONS

DISEASE OR PEST	Typical fruits attacked	What to watch out for	Suggested solutions to choose from
B. FUNGAL DISEASES			
HONEY FUNGUS *Hongo miel*	Stone and pip fruit trees	Sticky jelly-like lumps hanging from branches	* Spray with a fungicide including a neem/horsetail mix. * Cut out and burn badly affected branches that already show
RUST *Roya*	Raspberries, redcurrants and blackcurrants	Raised orange-brown pustules on leaves	* Spray with horsetail or neem late winter and early spring. * Dust with sulphur powder before fruit has formed.
	Grape vines	As above	* Plant rose bushes at end of rows.

C. NUTRITIONAL DISEASES

DISEASE OR PEST	Typical fruits attacked	What to watch out for	Suggested solutions to choose from
CLOROSIS *Citrus*	Citrus	Leaves go yellow, especially a problem in alkaline soils	* Feed with a dried blood product, e.g. Sequestrene. * If still young and in poor soil, dig up and replant after * working in plenty of well-rotted compost and manure (see section 4.10).

Notes:

* Potassium soap is now often referred as insecticidal soap and in Spain as *jabón negro*.

** Neem oil is produced from the kernels of the fruit of the neem tree *(Azadirachta indica)*. It is used as a general insecticide control on fruit trees, bushes and plants as well as on vegetables. For convenience it is often mixed with a safe emulsifier when mixing with water for use in a hand or back sprayer. Since neem is a soft insecticide modifying the reproductive life of pests, a cycle of several treatments is recommended.

Neem cake - what is left after the seeds are cold-pressed - can also be used to produce a dilute insecticidal concoction by mixing and leaving in cold water for a day. As well as spraying foliage, neem can be sprayed on the soil around fruit trees, bushes and plants to give some protection against insects and slugs. Until recently it was difficult to trace neem oil in Spain, but several companies now market products widely. If you have problems, ask your local horticultural shop or agricultural cooperative to go through their catalogues or computer data base. If you still draw a blank, you can obtain the products by mail order via www.trabe.net or www.niemhandel.de.

The neem tree is native to India and Burma but since its insecticidal, fungicidal and medicinal properties have been recognised it has been grown in Asia, West Africa, Central America and, more recently, the southern states of the USA. The tree survives best in poor, sandy, stony soils and can survive temperatures of 50 degrees C and drought conditions but will not tolerate frost or water-logged conditions. We managed to raise some samplings a few years ago but lost them during a winter frost. If you live on the Costa del Sol or Costa Tropical, you may manage to grow a tree to maturity. Normally, the tree fruits within five years and can live up to 200 years. The spring flowers are reminiscent of jasmine and we understand the pulp of the 2cm-long fruits can be eaten.

*** Nettle can be usefully added to neem sprays as it helps build up the immune system and the growth of stronger leaves.

**** Processionary caterpillars (lepidopteron/thumetopoea). If trying to remove them, do so with caution. Any skin contact with these caterpillars or their dust directly - or even indirectly by touching the tools used to collect them - can cause very nasty rashes and swellings on humans. Dogs have died after trying to eat them. They are best removed by using a pronged stick to pull the procession into a heap on top of sheets of newspaper, covering with more newspaper and setting alight. Add more paper and twigs until the caterpillars have been completedly burned (only do this on your own property in places where it is safe to light a small fire). They can also be exterminated by using a blow lamp, but only on a gravel path. To avoid risk of fire, do not do this in areas covered in grass or leaves. If the nests are high-up, it is dangerous to attempt to shoot them out of the tree as the caterpillars/dust from the nests can be distributed over a wide area. Better to watch carefully for the caterpillars descending the tree when they leave their nests and destroy them immediately they reach the ground.

We initially used the methods described in the table above with the exception of neem as it was extremely difficult to find anything vaguely organic. An organic orange grower introduced us to neem and we learned much more through a friend who had many Indian and American publications related to its use. It took some months to track down the product in Spain but luckily it is now widely distributed. Recent visits to the October Iberflora and Euroagro shows in Valencia have demonstrated that suppliers realise organic/natural solutions are a major growth market for both fruit and vegetable-growing and many commercial products are appearing based on potassium soap, garlic extracts, nettle extracts, comfrey extracts, neem and propolis. The latter we now use as a general fungicide.

Products labelled as organic, ecological or biological are now widely available in horticultural shops and from agricultural suppliers and agricultural cooperatives so there is no need for the domestic fruit-grower to use chemical products.

If you have problems locating these products, ask a local supplier to refer to *Eco-vad* by Carlos de Linan, Ediciones Agrotécnicas (www.agrotecnica.com). This publication describes a vast range of ecological insecticides, fungicides and fertilisers and their suppliers. The full range of inorganic products available is described in *Vademecum de productos fitosanitarios*, by the same author and also published by Agrotécnicas. Updated annually, these books can be obtained through the Casa del Libro (www.casadellibro.com), with branches in Madrid, Seville and Valencia.

PREPARATION OF NATURAL SPRAYS

There are two ways of preparing sprays, by making an infusion or a decoction.

An infusion is prepared by pouring boiling water over fresh or dried ingredients and then leaving to stand for 10 minutes before straining.

A decoction is prepared by bringing the ingredients and water to the boil and then simmering for 15 minutes before cooling and straining.

In each case it is preferable to use non-chlorinated water.

The natural sprays we have mentioned in the tables can be prepared as follows:

MAIN INGREDIENTS	MAIN USES	METHOD OF PREPARATION	DILUTIONS FOR USE
Potassium soap *Jabón potásico or Jabón negro*	Ecological washing-up liquid Spraying against insects such as aphids and mealy bugs etc. Also sooty leaves and other fungi caused by the sticky residue created by the above insects	Prepare immediately before use. Infusion of 50gr of soap in 1 litre of hot water. Mix well until soap fully dissolved.	1 to 10 with warm water. Stir well. Use immediately before it starts to cool and congeal.
Ecological washing-up liquid	As above	A few drops in 1 litre of cold water.	
Horsetail *Cola de caballo*	Spraying against fungal problems	Decoction of 100gr of fresh or 25grs of dried stems in 1.5 litres of water.	1 to 3 with cold water
Nettle *Ortigas*	Foliar feed and insecticide to build up defences of trees against insect and fungal attacks	**a.** Infusion of 100gr of fresh or 25grs of dried leaves in 1.5 litres of water. Allow to cool and leave overnight before straining and using.	1 to 20 with cold water
		b. Fill a bucket or barrel with freshly cut young nettles and cover with water. Put lid on and leave for one week before filtering and using.	As above
Garlic *Ajo*	Spraying against insect and fungal attacks	An infusion of 50gr crushed garlic in 1 litre of water. Cool and strain before use.	1 to 3 with cold water
Domestic bird-droppings, horsetail and nettle leaves	Spray against leaf curl	Dissolve 10gr of bird droppings (pigeon, budgerigar and other small birds) in a mix of 100cc of horsetail decoction and 100cc of nettle infusion	None

Interestingly, bottles of extracts of garlic, horsetail and nettle are now available commercially so these could be used as substitutes for the infusions and decoctions above. In which case, we suggest you use two or three drops in a litre of water.

Dried ingredients can be purchased from herb stalls in markets or health stores or they can be dried by yourself and stored for later use. It is better to prepare the above sprays each time you need them rather than storing for weeks in bottles. Cocktails of two or more of the sprays can be used as preventive sprays against both insects and fungal diseases.

5.8 AVOIDING ACCIDENTS IN YOUR FRUIT AND VEGETABLE GARDEN

Every year many accidents occur in gardens, especially in relation to the growing of fruit and vegetables. But most can be avoided by following safe gardening practices and taking care when designing, constructing and working in the garden. We base the following guidelines on our own experience and observations.

SAFE GARDEN PRACTICES

Always have a first aid kit in the house or garden shed. Check the contents and top up whenever used.

Avoid strains and sprains
• Warm up with a few light stretching exercises before starting heavy work especially in cold weather.
• Buy tools which are ergonomically designed.
• Use the right tool for the job especially when trying to prune thick branches and working heavy soils.
• Purchase small lightweight tools for children to use.
• Clean mud off tools, especially mattocks and spades to reduce the weight.
• Keep cutting edges of secateurs, saws and pruning chisels sharp to minimise effort.
• Avoid lifting heavy loads without help.
• Avoid overloading the wheelbarrow or the plastic buckets generally used by Spanish gardeners and builders.
• Wear a support belt to avoid hernias.
• Don't strain yourself by using an unnecessarily heavy watering can. Buy a smaller one especially for ladies and children.
• Don't mix too much mortar or concrete at any one time if constructing paths or the walls of raised beds etc.
• Don't try and work dried-out concrete like soil before moistening it or waiting for the next rains.
• Don't work waterlogged heavy soil until it dries out a little.
• Don't move heavy containers and sacks without a trolley or wheelbarrow.
• Wear a stomach-support belt if moving heavy loads.
• Don't overdo it by working long hours day after day especially in the midday sun.

Avoid dehydration

• Get used to wearing a sun hat.
• Always have a plastic bottle or earthenware pitcher of drinking water handy.
• In summer, work like the Spaniards, early and late.

Tools, equipment and machinery

• Purchase good tools, and keep them clean, oiled and sharpened as necessary.
• Buy tools with handle lengths appropriate to your height to avoid backache.
• Repair or replace any loose or broken handles or parts immediately.
• Ensure heads of mattocks etc. are tight. If the handle has dried out, soak in water to tighten it up before using.
• Don't leave sharp-edged tools lying around.
• Keep secateurs closed using the safety catches.
• Ensure that rungs, legs, rubber feet and catches on ladders and step ladders are safe.
• Use step-ladders and ladders when required. Don't risk your neck for the sake of spending a few minutes fetching the longer ladder.
• Ensure that guards and safety catches on machines are operable, secure and used.

• Have rotavators, strimmers, shredders and chainsaws regularly serviced.
• Ensure that electric leads are carefully laid out so that you don't trip over them or accidentally cut through them.
• Store fuel cans in a safe, secure, cool place.
• Don't allow young children to handle sharp and pointed tools.
• Avoid dangerous points and head-high obstacles.
• When pruning fruit trees don't leave dangerous ends at head height. Cut back to the trunk or main branches.
• Ensure that the ends of canes and posts are blunt or covered with tape to avoid eye injuries when leaning over or walking past.
• Don't swing canes around when working near others.
• Ensure that the ends of all wire ties are tied in tightly.
• Place scarecrows so that ends of the arms are not a danger to persons passing by.

• When pruning lower branches of large trees, don't train them at head height (too easy to walk into). It's better to keep the lowest branches at chest height or above the head of the tallest member of the family.

Tripping

• Don't leave unused tools, pruned branches, hoses, sheets of plastic or old carpets, canes, plastic netting, lengths of string and irrigation tubing around. Stack canes tidily in a drying rack. Take care when walking over damp plastic sheeting used for mulching and wet slippery soil.

Avoid using glass
· Use plastic sheeting rather than glass for cloches, garden frames and greenhouses.
· Use plastic rather than glass containers for storing seeds, irrigation system parts, etc.
· Don't take glass tumblers into the vegetable garden or orchard.
· Use plastic rather than glass bottles as insect traps.

Use ecological solutions
· Change from manufactured chemical fertilisers, insecticides, pesticides and fungicides to less hazardous natural/ecological/organic solutions.

Storage of fertilisers, insecticides, pesticides and fungicides
· Whether inorganic chemical or less hazardous organic/eco products, store in a secure place, preferably on high shelving or in locked bins away from pets and children.
· Ensure that all containers are sound with secure tops, no leakages and clear labels.
· Dispose of out-of-date products especially chemicals in the appropriate container at a local eco park.
· Wash out sprayers after use and before storage.
· Don't leave a sprayer full of chemicals around where someone could play with it.
· Don't leave empty canisters on the ground after use as one often sees around villages.

Protective clothing
· Wear appropriate protective clothing when handling fertilisers, insecticides, pesticides and herbicides and especially when spraying with chemicals.
· Purchase a good-quality protective hat, goggles, face mask, gloves and gardening shoes with reinforced toe caps. Builders merchants often sell the latter. Keep them clean and wash after handling chemicals. Disposable gloves and masks are a good idea when spraying.
· Always use tough-topped shoes when digging, raking, hoeing and using machines.
· Wear thick gloves when pruning prickly and spiky plants.
· Wear a protective mask and clothing when using a strimmer. Also goggles and gloves when using a shredder.

Pruning and felling
· Take care to keep fingers out of pruners, especially when holding something for pruning with the other hand.
· Knock pruning chisels upwards and away from you.
· Fell dying trees and cut off dangerous branches before they fall.
· Take special care when cutting off and carrying date palm fronds. Avoid the spikes at any cost.

Animals and stinging insects
• Locate and destroy the nests of wasps, hornets and processionary caterpillars and lines of processionary caterpillars when they come out of the trees.
• Watch out for and avoid scorpions, adders, processionary caterpillars and biting spiders.
• Have an onion, garlic clove or cider vinegar handy for rubbing on bites.
• Wear a natural insect repellent.

Control use of bonfires
• Only use when essential. Compost as much vegetable and fruit waste as possible, except citrus fruits which are too acidic. Put the latter in the waste collection bin.
• Shred prunings of fruit trees and bushes and add to the compost heap or put in eco bins. As a last resort use a skip.
• If you do have a bonfire, first obtain the necessary local licence and follow local safety by-laws.
• Control the size of bonfires by burning in an oil drum or breeze-block screen. One often sees the latter being used in orange groves.
• Don't leave a bonfire unattended. Always have a hosepipe or buckets of water nearby so as to bring back under control fierce or spreading fires.
• Put out and dampen down any fire before leaving it.

Wash vegetables and fruit
• Wash all sprayed vegetables and fruit before cooking or eating raw.

DESIGN AND CONSTRUCTION

Cane supports
• Ensure that supports for beans etc. are firmly tied and guyed.

Walls, fences and supports
• Ensure that walls to which any fruit trees or bushes are tied are on secure foundations and sufficiently strong to withstand the forces from the plants themselves, gale-force winds, the vibrations of passing lorries, etc.
• Ensure that retaining walls below vegetable plots or around raised beds are strong and stable enough to support the infill behind, especially during or after heavy rains.
• Ensure that retaining walls and boundary walls have enough drainage pipes to allow the pressure of retained water to be relieved.
• Ensure that dry stone walls are wide enough and sufficiently well-stacked to withstand their own weight and the weight of retained earth. Also that the top stones are cemented to make them safe to stand on.
• Ensure that post and wire supports for fruit bushes and vines are secure.

Paths and terraces
• Build paths through and around vegetable plots and orchards with non-slip surfaces.
• Ensure easy slopes and steps for all ages.

• Regularly clean off the winter build-up of slippery algae and moss, especially under trees.
• Repair as soon as they occur loose slabs and cracks that could cause trips.

Steps
• Construct with equal rises and treads to reduce risk of tripping.
• Ensure the edges of treads are totally secure. Loose and broken edges can be lethal.
• Use non-slip materials. Clean off any mud and moss that builds up.
• Install handrails alongside if there are aged, infirm or handicapped persons in the family.

Electricity
• Install a separate trip for the garden circuit.
• Use armoured cables and strong plastic conduits. Sink them a minimum of 20cm-deep and cover with slabs or concrete. Mark where they are so as not to inadvertently dig down with a fork, spade, pick axe or mattock.
• Use special waterproof fittings and immediately change anything damaged.
• Use a qualified electrician.
• Switch off jammed machines before attempting to unblock or clear.
• Always get professionals to dismantle and service electrically powered machines.
• Don't use electrically powered equipment in the rain.

Ponds to attract beneficial wildlife
• Fence off or cover when young children are around.
• Ensure surrounding terrace and rocks are secure.
• Store pond chemicals securely.

Rock surrounded pond

5.9 ASSESSING AND IMPROVING YOUR RESULTS

ARE YOU PLEASED WITH YOUR HARVESTS OF FRUIT?

Each autumn or spring ask yourself how well you did with your fruit-growing and what could be improved during the next year? For starters, ask yourself:

Are we enjoying harvests of ripe, tasty home-grown fruit on most days of the year?

Have we produced it in the most natural, ecological and organic manner possible?

If we are not satisfied or have had problems, what can we do about it?

What additional fruit trees, bushes, vines or plants should we plant to achieve a more continuous succession of fruit crops throughout the year?

What fruit trees, bushes and plants were not successful and are best dug up and replaced?

The two self-audits that follow are designed to help you answer the above questions. You can learn from your relative successes and failures and plan to do even better next year.

HOW NATURAL/ECOLOGICAL/ORGANIC HAVE YOU BECOME?

We suggest you complete the audit once a year. Add up your scores and compare with the observations of scores provided below the box.

Don't be disappointed if you start with a low score. The audit and earlier sections of the book will indicate where you can make a few changes over the next 12 months.

BEST PRACTICE	HOW WOULD YOU DESCRIBE YOUR CURRENT PERSONAL PRACTICES?	SCORE FOR ANSWER	PERSONAL SCORE
1. Improve the structure and fertility of the soil using only natural/ ecological materials.	1.1 Only use proprietary inorganic chemical fertilisers.	0	
	1.2 Use above plus peat and peat substitutes.	1	
	1.3 Now use some compost and have cut back on the use of chemical fertilisers by half.	2	
	1.4 Use well-rotted manure and compost but may include some non-organic materials.	3	
	1.5 Only use well-rotted manure and compost from organic sources.	4	
	1.6 As above plus the use of seaweed.	5	
2. Self-production of the materials used for enriching the soil and producing natural feeds.	2.1 Buy proprietary mixes in bags.	0	
	2.2 Buy in bags but have started a small compost heap.	1	
	2.3 Have a large compost heap and have reduced what is purchased.	2	
	2.4 Have two compost heaps, a source of well-rotted manure and use, some compost from local eco park.	3	
	2.5 As above, but now have a few rabbits, guinea pigs and hens that produce useful manures.	4	
	2.6 Have purchased a few sheep and goats that keep the orchard tidy. Now totally self sufficient from own animals, birds, compost heaps and productive wormery.	5	
3. Feed crops with natural/ecological plant feeds when essential during the growing season.	3.1 Use only proprietary inorganic, manufactured chemical feeds.	0	
	3.2 Still use above but have started to use proprietary organic/ecological feeds.	1	
	3.3 Use mainly proprietary feeds but have started to prepare own.	2	
	3.4 Use only own produced feeds but not sure that all manure used is organic.	3	
	3.5 As 3.4 with all organic manures and plants but only feed the soil.	4	
	3.6 Have a planned programme for using a variety of own organic feeds as soil and foliage feeds.	5	

BEST PRACTICE	HOW WOULD YOU DESCRIBE YOUR CURRENT PERSONAL PRACTICES?	SCORE FOR ANSWER	PERSONAL SCORE
4. Use non-chemical methods of weed control.	**4.1.** Regularly use herbicides.	0	
	4.2 Leave to grow. Previous year's fallen fruit fertilise following year's growth. Weed kill if it gets out of hand.	1	
	4.3 Stopped using weed-killers. Strim orchard twice a year. Soil rather hard as a result.	2	
	4.4 Rotavate twice a year but catch on shallow roots.	3	
	4.5 Keep inner orchard clear by hoeing and shallow rotavating. Leave ring of companion plants to attract beneficial insects.	4	
	4.6 Have mulched under all trees with chippings over woven plastic sheeting but have left patches of wild flowers to attract beneficial insects.	5	
5. Use natural/ ecological insect deterrents and pesticides and companion planting for pest/disease prevention and control.	**5.1** Still use chemical sprays. No companion planting.	0	
	5.2 80% chemical, 20% natural.	1	
	5.3 60% chemical, 40% natural, started companion planting.	2	
	5.4 20% chemical, 80% natural, and much more companion planting.	3	
	5.5 Only proprietary and some own natural sprays, substantial companion plantings and starting to grow naturally.	4	
	5.6 Only own natural plant sprays and sulphur used but extent very much reduced as natural predators, extensive companion planting and growing naturally solve most problems.	5	
6. Plant ecologically/ organically grown fruit trees, bushes and plants.	**6.1** Just buy the first seen.	0	
	6.2 Only now realise that you can purchase them.	1	
	6.3 Have realised the benefit and searching for a grower.	2	
	6.4 Have located an organic grower and ordered some for the next planting season,.	3	
	6.5 Half are now certified.	4	
	6.6 All are certified officially as having been grown organically.	5	

BEST PRACTICE	HOW WOULD YOU DESCRIBE YOUR CURRENT PERSONAL PRACTICES?	SCORE FOR ANSWER	PERSONAL SCORE
7. Watering and feeding are restricted to the levels required to produce natural-sized, healthy, juicy, fruits rather than forced watery-tasteless fruits.	7.1 Never do either. Trees do show signs of regular stress, some have died.	0	
	7.2 Water and fertilise copiously hoping for bigger fruit but major fruit falls and fungal problems and some trees dying.	1	
	7.3 Have cut back feeding and watering but problems still occur.	2	
	7.4 Recognise problem and using dilute natural feeds in irrigation water. Fruit rarely falls but still have root and trunk fungal problems.	3	
	7.5 Have a set computerised programme of watering and feeding year-in, year-out.	4	
	7.6 Monitor the needs and effects of watering. Mature trees rarely show signs of needing more. Rarely feed and have marvellous crops.	5	
8. Development/ management of naturally balanced eco-system.	8.1 Plot is sterile. No sign of wildlife or earthworms. Land gets waterlo-gged and have to live with fungal problems.	0	
	8.2 Occasionally see a bird and odd insect.	1	
	8.3 Birds visit and live off insect population.	2	
	8.4 Birds resident and nest. Obviously more natural food available. Nets protect vulnerable fruit when it starts to ripen.	3	
	8.5 Orchard now a haven of wildlife. Birds and beneficial insects control pests to acceptable level if they appear. Good drainage and clean soil surface prevents fungal diseases. Nets rarely necessary.	4	
	8.6 As above and have a number of sheep or goats to keep the orchard tidy.	5	

OBSERVATIONS ON FRUIT AUDIT SCORES

31-40. You have become a full and competent ecological/organic and natural-fruit grower and have probably searched out some fruit trees, bushes and plants certified as having been grown organically (not easy in Spain).

21-30. You are obviously well on the way to becoming a dedicated organic gardener, very conscious of the needs of natural and ecological practices.

11-20. You appear to believe in the benefits of moving towards growing your fruit naturally, ecologically and organically and are starting to make progress.

0- 10. You have obviously not yet seen the benefits. We suggest you re-read Part One and consider starting to change some of your practices during the next 12 months.

WHAT CAN YOU LEARN FROM LAST YEAR'S CROP SUCCESSES AND FAILURES?

Growing fruit in Spain, as in any country, is an everlasting learning process. But especially so here because many of the fruits, soils, seasons and climate will be different to those experienced before you came to Spain. Most importantly the weather in late winter/early spring when trees are in bud or just in blossom often fluctuates dramatically. One day it's hot, encouraging buds to swell and flowers to form fruit, and then overnight freezing gales demolish the best display of blossom for years. For us an apricot tree is the most vulnerable so the good years when this does not happen are especially precious.

It makes good sense to reflect on your successes and failures during the past year before finalising your action plan and making any additional plantings of fruit trees, bushes or plants. The following questions will help you do this systematically.

Which fruit crops did you most enjoy and are there varieties you should plant more of and others perhaps replace?

Which crops were the greatest successes in terms of flavour, sweetness, aroma, bite, yields and lack of problems?

Why do you consider them as successes?

Were these crops also among your greatest successes during the previous year?

What crops were your greatest failures and why?

Were they among your greatest failures the previous year?

Can you think of any fundamental reason why some fruit crops did worse than others?

What were the differences in the ways you grew the best and poorest crops?

The preparation of the soil before planting? Source, variety, age and certification of the trees and plants? When and how you planted them? Where you planted them and their exposure to winds, rain, hail and snow?

Have you taken into account:

> • The pattern of sun and rain and day and night temperatures and nights when the frost factor temperature was well below the temperature on the thermometer?
>
> • The way you dealt with weeds and the frequency of rotavating or hoeing the ground under trees, bushes and vines?
>
> • The way in which plants were staked, tied or supported on wires, or planted through plastic?
>
> • The extent of companion plantings to attract beneficial insects?
>
> • Whether you grew strips of vegetables between the rows of trees?
>
> • Whether you planted or pruned trees, bushes and vines on preferential days according to the lunar calendar?
>
> • The extent of pest or disease damage, the extent to which you had to use insecticides and fungicides? Were they ecological/organic?

Overall, what did you change from previous years when the poor crops or similar crops were more successful? What did you forget or not have time to do thoroughly?

Most importantly, should you change your approach to growing fruit and when should you start to make the changes?

PART SIX

A FRUIT-GROWING CALENDAR

The calendar is presented in two-monthly periods, i.e. January-February, March-April etc. This is to accommodate regional and altitude variations in seasonal microclimates and recognises that, for most persons with busy lives, a more precise calendar of events will be too complex.

JANUARY/FEBRUARY: winter
MARCH/APRIL: spring
MAY/JUNE: late spring/early summer
JULY/AUGUST: summer
SEPTEMBER/OCTOBER: late summer/early autumn
NOVEMBER/DECEMBER: late autumn/early winter

JANUARY/FEBRUARY

1. Winter pruning of fruit trees.
2. Burn diseased wood or send to incinerator.
3. Keep the best prunings as pea and bean sticks for the vegetable garden.
4. Winter oil wash of summer fruiting trees and fix grease/glue bands if not done before end of year.
5. Clean up all leaves and fallen fruit under deciduous fruit trees and compost. Don't compost evergreen leaves or fallen citrus fruits as they are too acidic for the compost heap.
6. Clean up strawberry beds and put mats and straw under plants to hold young fruit above the ground.
7. Plant new strawberry plants if not done in November or December.
8. Cut out dead raspberry canes and cut back new growth by a third. Then give a feed high in potash.
9. Tighten training wires for raspberries and cordon and espalier trees. Tie up tall raspberry canes and trees as necessary.
10. Prune currant bushes. Then give them a feed high in potash.
11. Spray citrus trees with insecticide before flowering.
12. Weed around bushes and trees.
13. In frost-free areas plant new fruit trees and bushes.
14. Construct wire supports for vines and cordon and fan trees.
15. Spray fruit trees with neem fortnightly.
16. Plant garlic around nectarine, peach and cherry trees to help guard against leaf curl and other fungal diseases.

17. Prune grape vines and give them a light dusting of sulphur powder.

18. Clean out insect traps and refill with bait.

19. Sort through and clean up collection of fertilisers and sprays.

20. Give comfrey plants a dressing of chicken manure or another nitrogen feed.

MARCH/APRIL

1. Thin out non-fruiting and crossing branches on fruit trees.

2. Fix traps for leaf miner moth on citrus trees.

3. Cut out any frost damage on citrus and semi tropical/tropical fruits.

4. Give frost-damaged trees a foliar nitrogen feed.

5. In March give fruit trees a general feed.

6. Give strawberries a feed and put straw under forming fruit.

7. Clean up banana plants and use leaves as a mulch high in potassium.

8. Start to dust grape vines with sulphur.

9. Mulch raspberries with well-rotted compost and manure.

10. Spray raspberries and other soft fruit bushes with neem.

11. Give all trees and plants a good soak if there are no spring rains.

12. Watch for early leaf curl and spray.

13. Continue to spray fruit trees with neem fortnightly.

14. Plant new kiwi and grape vines.

15. Plant new citrus trees and others if not planted last autumn.

16. Thin out flowering branches of mature citrus trees.

17. Prune carob trees to shape if not done earlier.

18. Spring rotavation under/around fruit trees.

19. Sow or plant melons in mild areas. In cooler areas raise plantlets ingreenhouse.

20. Raise golden berry plantlets in greenhouse.

MAY/JUNE

1. Harvest late oranges and mandarins.
2. Thin out forming fruit on citrus, peach, plum and nectarine trees to stimulate larger fruits.
3. Enjoy the first harvests of raspberries.
4. Spray peach and nectarines against leaf curl.
5. Plant sub-tropical fruit trees.
6. Clean up early fallen fruits such as apricots and cherries.
7. Rotovate all growth under trees into soil.
8. Plant out young bananas and papaya plants.
9. Thin out bunches of grapes and cut out excess non fruiting growth on vines and continue to dust with sulphur.
10. Water citrus trees to swell the fruit.
11. Freeze or make jams with surplus strawberries, currants, cherries and apricots.
12. Feed and water kiwi, blackberry and loganberry vines.
13. Watch out for slugs and snails on strawberries, raspberries and currant bushes.
14. Watch out for snails on citrus trees.
15. Fit or check the protection tubes on young citrus trees.
16. Check joints and sprays on irrigation system.
17. Increase level of irrigation as temperatures increase.
18. Spray with neem against moths and flies.
19. Place bags over peaches to protect from insects.
20. Bottle some cherries in syrup or kirsch.

JULY/AUGUST

1. Continue to dust grapes lightly with sulphur. Dust also with copper sulphate if it rains as fruit swells and colours.
2. Keep cleaning up any fallen fruit.
3. Hoe summer weeds under fruit trees.
4. Harvest almonds, separate shells and dry in sun before storing.
5. Harvest and freeze or bottle surplus peaches and nectarines.
6. Prepare a jar of mixed fruits in brandy or rum for Christmas.
7. Harvest pears and last of plums.
8. Dry spare grapes as raisins.
9. Summer prune apples and pear trees.
10. Ensure you water kiwis, papayas, bananas and mangos copiously.
11. Water and feed raspberries and strawberries to stimulate autumn fruiting.
12. Put wasp traps around fig trees.
13. Don't worry about your almond tree losing leaves - this is normal.
14. Ensure citrus trees don't dry out especially if in pots.
15. Thin out oranges and mandarins to increase size of fruit on small trees.
16. Give fruit trees a summer spray of neem or potassium soap solution against Mediterranean fruit fly and moths.
17. Spray likewise the soil and undergrowth around trees.
18. Watch out for and treat mealy bugs and woolly aphids on citrus trees.
19. Start to clear up fallen leaves.
20. Spray olives with neem.

SEPTEMBER/OCTOBER

1. Harvest apples and persimmons and tray for storage.
2. Harvest grapes and start home-made wine.
3. Harvest sloes, blackberries and prickly pears and bottle with anis for a winter tipple.
4. Harvest blackberries. Freeze surplus or bottle with anis.
5. Harvest apples and pears and store in cool, dry place.
6. Give fruit trees an autumn feed.
7. Prune out excess growth from kiwi vines.
8. Prepare ground for new fruit trees and bushes.
9. Plant out new strawberry runners and remove old plants.
10. Cut back bananas after fruiting.
11. Pick quince and make jelly.
12. Pick some early mandarins.
13. Pick excess lemons and store in cool cellar or fridge.
14. Freeze last raspberries for Christmas.
15. Harvest chestnuts, hazel nuts, pecan nuts, pistachios, walnuts and dry before storing.
16. Dig up, wash and dry peanuts.
17. Harvest last of melons for storing.
18. Give fruit trees a fortnightly spray with neem.
19. Start to harvest mandarins and clementines.
20. Clean up fallen leaves and fruit.

NOVEMBER/DECEMBER

1. Plant new kiwi vines and fruit bushes.
2. Harvest first olives and prepare for pickling in brine.
3. Harvest bananas for Christmas.
4. Plant bare-rooted or container deciduous fruit trees.
5. Cover strawberries with cloches to force for winter fruit.
6. Start to harvest first tangerines and oranges.
7. Plant new raspberry canes or transplant a new row of suckers.
8. Prune currant bushes and blackberry and loganberry vines.
9. Weed around strawberries and raspberries.
10. Mulch along raspberry rows.
11. Harvest last persimmons and store.
12. Protect avocado, papaya and mango trees from frost and cold winds.
13. Tie up banana leaves in fleece if in an exposed situation.
14. Fix grease bands round the trunks of fruit trees.
15. Check that stakes and ties on young fruit trees are firm.
16. Clean and check that all pruners are in working order. Change springs and sharpen blades if necessary.
17. Check, oil and overhaul, if necessary, the strimmer ready to recycle all rubbish from the winter cutback of the flower and fruit garden to compost heaps.
18. Hang new insect traps on fruit trees.
19. Sweep or rake up the last of the fallen leaves and fruit and put on compost heap.
20. Prepare ground for spring planting of citrus and other tender fruit trees.

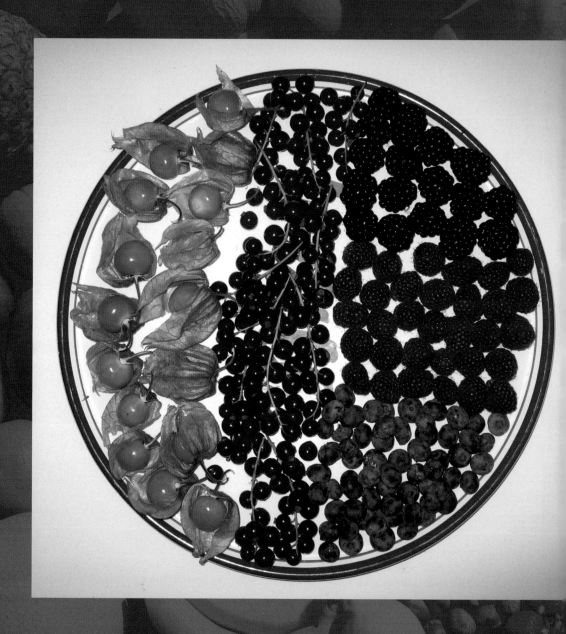

VOCABULARY AND INDEX

This comprehensive gardening English–Spanish vocabulary, designed to help you grow fruit, includes the names of all the fruit trees and technical terms used in this book.

The Vocabulary includes the following sections.

The main Index commences on page 209

VOCABULARY

Trees, bushes, plants (in brackets name of the fruit)

almond: *almendro* (almendra)
apple: *manzano* (manzana)
apple, crab: *manzano silvestre* (manzana)
apricot: *albaricoquero* (albaricoque)
avocado: *aguacate* (aguacate)
banana palm: *platanera* (plátano)
blackberry: *zarza* (zarzamora, mora)
blackcurrant: *grosellero negro* (grosella negra)
calamondino: *calamondinero*
Cape gooseberry: *physalis*
carob: *algarrobo* (algarroba)
cherry: *cerezo* (cereza)
chestnut: *castaño* (castaña)
clementine: *clementina*
custard apple: *chirimoyo* (chirimoya)
date palm: *palmera* (dátil)
fig: *higuera* (higo)
gooseberry: *grosellero espinoso* (grosella espinosa, uva espina)
grapefruit: pomelo
grapevine: vid
guava: guayaba
hazel: *avellano* (avellana)
jujube: *azufaifo* (azufaifa)
kiwi: kiwi
kiwini: kiwini
kumquat: naranja china
lemon: *limonero* (limón)
lime: *limero* (lima)
limequat: lima china
loganberry: *frambueso norteamericano* (frambuesa norteamericana)
loquat: *níspero de Japón, dulce*
lychee: *lychee*
macadamia: macadamia
mandarin: *mandarino* (mandarina)
mango: *mango* (mango)
medlar: *níspero europeo, de invierno*
melon: melón
mulberry: *morera* (mora)
nectarine: nectarina
olive: *olivo* (oliva, aceituna)
orange: *naranjo* (naranja)
orange, bitter (fruit): naranja cajel
papaya: *papayo* (papaya)
paraguaya: *paraguayo* (paraguaya)
passion fruit: pasionaria
passion fruit flower: granadilla
peach: *melocotonero* (melocotón)
peanut: cacahuete
pear: *peral* (pera)

pecan: pacana
persimmon: caqui
pine nut: piñón
pistachio: pistacho
plum: *ciruelo* (ciruela)
pomegranate: *granado* (granada)
quince: *membrillero* (membrillo)
raspberry: *frambueso* (frambuesa)
redcurrant: grosellero rojo
rhubarb: ruibarbo
satsuma: satsuma
strawberry (large, cultivated): fresón
strawberry, Alpine: fresa
strawberry tree: madroño
walnut: *nogal* (nuez)
water melon: sandía

Useful words

allotment: huerto
bed, cultivated: bancal
garden: jardín
garden, vegetable: huerto
garden, fruit: jardín frutero
gardener: jardinero
bonfire: hoguera
climate, macro: macroclima
climate, micro: microclima
climate, nano: nanoclima
cloche: campana de cristal/plástico para proteger plantas
cloche, tunnel: túnel de plástico
companion plant: planta beneficiosa acompañante
composter: compostador
compost heap: montón de abono vegetal, pila de compuestos, pila de compostaje
container: contenedor
copse: bosquecillo
diet: dieta
disease: enfermedad
diversity: diversidad
drainage: drenaje
drought: sequía
fence: cerca, vallado
flower bed: cuadro, macizo, lecho de flores
frost, air: escarcha del aire
frost, ground: escarcha
fruit: fruta
fruit tree: árbol frutal
furrow: surco
garden frame: mini invernadero
gardening, vegetables: horticultura
greenhouse: invernadero

grow bag: saco para cultivar
gutter: gotera, canal
hail: granizo
hedge: seto
hole: hoyo
hose: manguera
house: casa
injury: herida
insect: insecto
irrigation system: sistema de riego
ladder, step: escala
lawn: césped
moon/lunar calendar: calendario lunar
mound, earth: montón de tierra
mulch: alcolchado
nature: naturaleza
orchard: huerto de frutales
path: vereda/senda
patio: patio
pergola: pérgola
pest: plaga
plant: planta
plantlet: plántula
plant pot: maceta
pollination: polinización
pond: estanque
property: propiedad
rain: lluvia
rain, to: llover
rainwater: agua de lluvia
raised bed: macizo elevado
ridge: caballón
rockery: jardín de roca
row: hilera
seat: silla
seed bed: semillero
seed box: caja de simientes
shade: sombra
shed, garden: cobertizo
shrubbery: arbustos
slope: cuesta, pendiente
smallholding with house: finca
smallholding without house: parcela
snow: nieve
strip plot: huerto estrecho
sun: sol
terrace (cultivated): terraza, bancal
tub: cubeta
ten-tub vegetable garden: huerta de diez
    cubetas
tie: atadura
tools, garden: útiles de jardinería
trellis: enrejado
view: vista
water: agua
water butt: tina/barril para agua
waterway, channel: canal, acequia
watering-can: regadera
wall: muro
watering system: sistema de riego
weather: tiempo

wildlife: fauna
windbreak: abrigada, cortavientos
wormery: vermicompostador
worm: lombriz
yard: patio, corral

Materials

bag: saco
basket: capacho, cesta
bottle: botella
box: caja
bucket: cubo
cane: caña
chippings: gravilla suelta
compost: abono vegetal
face mask: mascarilla
fertiliser: abono
fertiliser, foliar: abono foliar
fertiliser, granular: abono granulado
fertiliser, soluble: abono soluble
fleece: malla térmica, fleece
fungicide: fungicida
gloves: guantes
goggles: lentes protectoras
grit: cascajo, grava
handle, spare: manga disponible
herbicide: herbicida
insecticide: insecticida
labels, plastic: etiquetas de plástico
manure: estiércol
mulch: mantillo
netting: red
peat: turba
pesticide: pesticida
Ph meter: contador de Ph
post: poste
rock: roca
sack: saco
sand: arena
sheet plastic (solid): hoja de plástico
sheet plastic (woven): malla de plástico
slab of rock: bloque
soil: suelo, tierra
stake: rodriga, estaca
string: cuerda
thermometer: termómetro
timer: interruptor horario
water: agua
wax: cera
weedkiller: herbicida
wire: alambre
wood: madera
worm, earth: lombriz
worm compost: humus de lombriz

Tools

axe: hacha
blower/vacuum cleaner: aspiradora
broom: escoba
bucket: cubo
bucket (basket-like): capacho
cane: caña
chisel: escoplo
dibber: plantador, almocafre
dryer: secadora
duster (see powder blower)
fork: horca
funnel: embudo
grafting tape: cinta de injertar
hammer: mortillo
handle, spare: mango disponible
harrow: grada
hedge trimmer: recortador de setos
hoe: azadón, peta
hose: manguera
knife: cuchillo
mallet: mazo
mattock: azadón, pico
multi-headed tool: herramienta de multi-cabeza
pick axe: pico azado
pipe, plastic: tubo plástico
pliers: alicates
plough: arado
powder blower: espolvoreador
pruners, extendable: tijeras de podar
    extensibles
rake: rastrillo
ridging rake: bilbadora, rastrillo de caballones
rotavator: moto azada, retovato
saw: sierra
secateurs: tijeras de podar
scissors: tijeras
sharpening stone: piedra de afilar
shovel: pala grande
shredder: trituradora
sieve: criba
sledge hammer: mazo
sock: calcetín
stocking: media
spade: pala
sprayer: pulverizadora
sprinkler: rociadera
step-ladder: escalera de tijera
strimmer: desbrozadora
swoe: azada
tank: cisterna
teaspoon: cucharilla
tool: herramienta
trowel: desplantador, palustre
watering-can: regadera
weeder: escardera
weed extractor: extractor de malas hierbas
wheelbarrow: carretilla
water pump: bomba para agua

Parts of plants

bark: corteza
blossom: flores
branch: rama
bud: brote
bud (flower): capullo
bud (leaf): yema
cutting: esqueje
flower: flor
flower head: cabezuela
fruit: fruta
graft: injerto
leaf: hoja
perfume: perfume
plantlet: plántula
pollen: polen
root: raíz
seed: semilla
seed head: cabezuela
seedling: plántula
spray of flowers: ramita
stem: tallo
string of onions/garlic: ristra de cebollas/ ajos
texture: textura
trunk: tronco
twig: ramita

Types of plants

annual: anual
bamboo: bambú
bulb: bulbo
cactus: cactus
climber: trepadora
corm: bulbo
creeper: enredadera
fruit tree: frutal
grass: hierba
ground cover: cubierto por el terreno
house plant: planta de interior
herb: hierba aromática
palm: palma, palmera
perennial: perenne
rambler: enredadera
shrub: arbusto
succulent: suculento
tree: árbol
tree (evergreen): árbol de hoja perenne
tree (deciduous): árbol de hoja caduca
vegetable (green): verdura
vegetable (general): hortaliza
vegetable (pulses): legumbres
variety: variedad
vine, grape: vid
weed: mala hierba

Gardening verbs

axe: hachear, dar hachazos
bear fruit: dar fruto, frutar
bloom, flower: florecer
brush up: cepillar
build: construir
burn: quemar
bury: enterrar
buy: comprar
cascade: caer en cascada
change: cambiar
choose: elegir
clean up: limpiar
climb: subir
connect: conectar
cook: cocinar
construct: construir
cover over: cubrir
create: crear
cultivate: cultivar
cut: cortar
cut back: recortar
cut down: talar
dampen: mojar, humedecer
deadhead: descabezar
decide: decidir
design: diseñar
develop: desarrollar
die: morir
dilute: diluir
dig: cavar
dig a hole: excavar
dig in: añadir al suelo
dig over: recavar
dig up: desarraigar
distill: destilar
divide: dividir
do: hacer
drip: gotear
dry: secar
eat: comer
earth up: tomar caballón de tierra
employ: emplear
empty: vaciar
emulsify: emulsionar
enjoy: divertirse
fertilise: fertilizar
fill in: rellenar
flood: inundar
force: forzar
garden (general): trabajar en el jardín
garden (work on vegetable plot): cultivar
   el huerto
graft: injertar
grow (a fruit): cultivar
grow (process of): crecer
hammer: clavar
harrow: gradar
harvest: recoger

hoe: azadonar
identify: identificar
irrigate: regar, irrigar
label: etiquetar
level: nivelar
line: alinear
kill off: exterminar
maintain: mantener
mark: señalar, marcar
maximise (something): sacar el máximo
   partido (a algo)
measure: medir
minimise: minimizar
mix: mezclar
mix in something: añadir algo
mow: cortar
open: abrir
pinch out: quitar con los dedos
plan: planear
plant: plantar
plough: arar
pollinate: polinizar, fecundar
pour: echar
propagate: propagar
protect: proteger
prune: podar
pump: bombear
rain: llover
rake: rastrillar
ridge: caballonar
rotate, crops: cultivar en rotación
rotavate: trabajar con motorcultor, roturar
saw: serrar
select: escoger
separate: apartar
screen: tapar
shade: proteger del sol
shake up: agitar
sharpen: afilar
sieve: cribar
shear: cortar
shred: triturar
shelter: resguardar
snow: nevar
soak: remojar
sort out: clasificar, separar
sow: sembrar
spray: pulverizar, rociar
spread: extender
sprinkle: rociar
stake: rodrigar
start, motor: arrancar
stimulate: estimular
stir: agitar
strim: desbrozar
sweep up: barrer
take out: quitar
thin out: entresacar
tidy up: arreglar
tie up: atar
till: labrar

top up: llenar
train: guiar, dirigir
transplant: trasplantar
trench (to dig): excavar
turn on: abrir
turn off: cerrar
turn over: volver
turn (rotate): girar
use: usar
water: regar
weed: desherbar, escardar, sacar las malas hierbas
weigh: pesar
wet: mojar
wilt: marchitar

Gardening adjectives

colourful: lleno de color vivo
bright: brillante
burnt: quemado
by the hour: por hora
chemical: químico
clammy: pegajoso
clayey: arcilloso
cloudy: nublado
cold: frío
comfortable: cómodo
cool: fresco
cosy: acogedor
damp, humid: húmedo
dappled: moteado
dead: muerto
dry: seco
drying: secando
dull: sombrío
dying: moribundo
early: temprano
ecological: ecológico
firm: firme
flooded: inundado
flowery: florido
free-draining: de drenaje libre
frost-bitten: congelado
frosty: de helada, escarchado
frozen: congelado
going to seed: granando
grafted: injertado
growing: creciendo
healthy: sano
heirloom: reliquia de familia
heritage: herencia
hot (climate): cálido
hot (weather): calor
infested: plagado
in flower: floreciente
in fruit: con fruto
juicy: jugoso
level: a nivel
late: tarde, último
liquid: líquido

muddy: lodoso, embarrado
natural: natural
organic: orgánico/ecológico
inorganic: inorgánico
perfumed: perfumado, aromático
powdered: en polvo
prickly: espinoso, con pinchos
rainy: lluvioso
ripe: maduro
rotting: podrido
sandy: arenoso
seasonal: estacional
season, early: temprano
season, mid: medio
season, late: tardío
shady: sombreado
sharp: afilado
sheltered: abrigado
short: corto
sloping: inclinado
spiky: puntiagudo
stunted: enano
sunny: soleado
sub-tropical: sub-tropical
tall: alto
temperate: templado
tropical: tropical
unripe: inmaduro, verde
young: joven
warm: cálido
water: agua
waterlogged: anegado
water supply: abastecimiento de agua
watery: acuoso
windy: ventoso
wilted/withered: marchito

Measurements

pulgada: inch
pie (.308 metres): foot
metro: metre
area: 100 square metres
hanegada (traditional measurement used in Valencia and other regions): 833.33 square metres
fanega, fanegada (measurements used in Andalusia): 64 areas, 6460 square metres, 1.59 acres
hectare: 10,000 square metres
acre (.405 hectares or 4047 square metres): acre
arroba: 25 pounds
kilo: 2.2 pounds
1000 kilos, tonelada métrica: metric ton
litro: 1.76 pints
cubo lleno: bucketful

INDEX